Mystic Garden Vol. 2

![cat flower illustration]

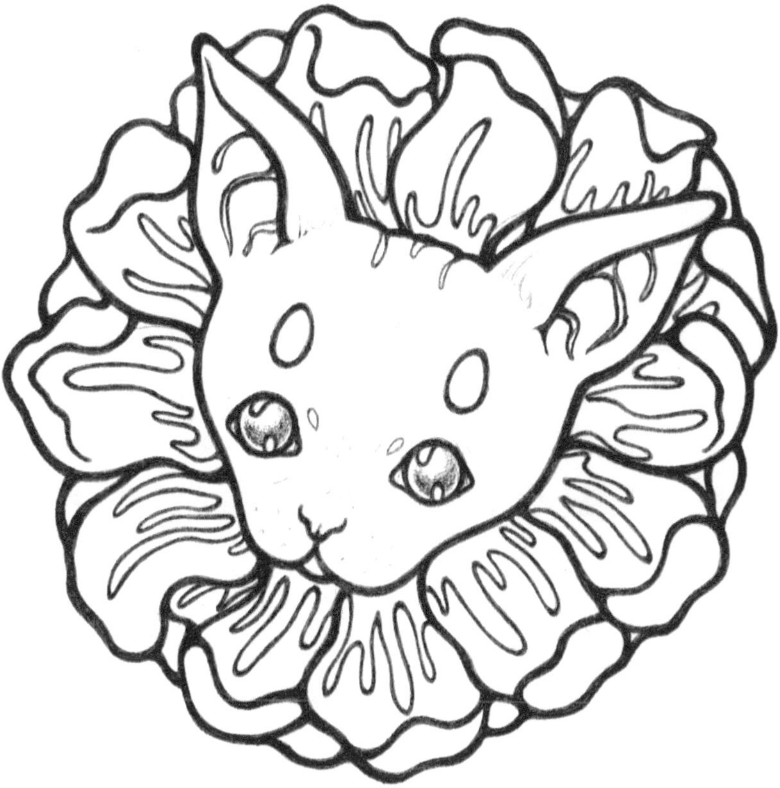

Sara Hopkins

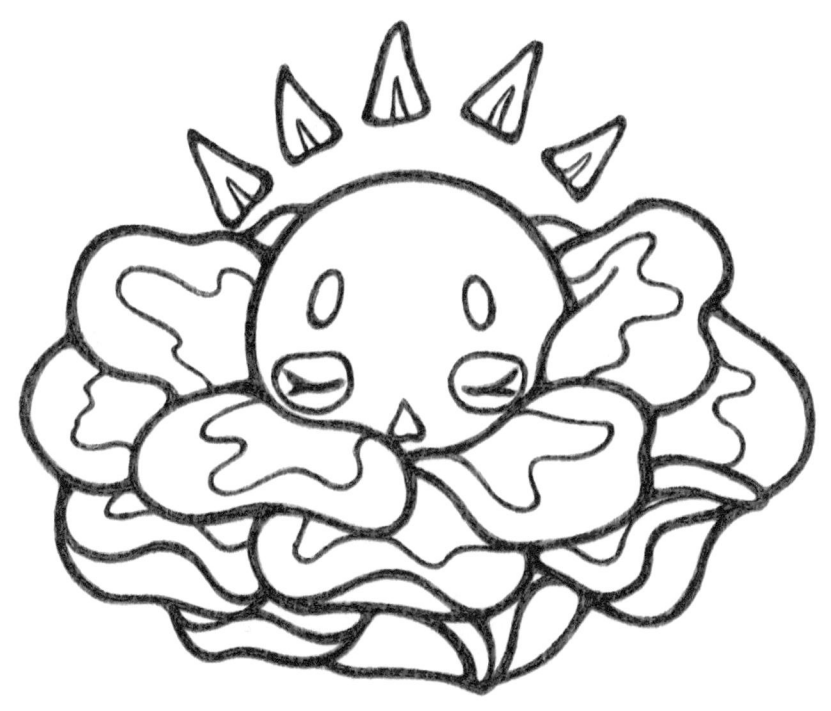

Cute, creepy, and sometimes a little weird. I hope you enjoy these drawings and have fun coloring them. Thank you for supporting small artists and validating what we do. It means more than most of us can express. Thank you for your encouragement!
Share your work with me
@sarahopkinsart
<3
Love, Sara

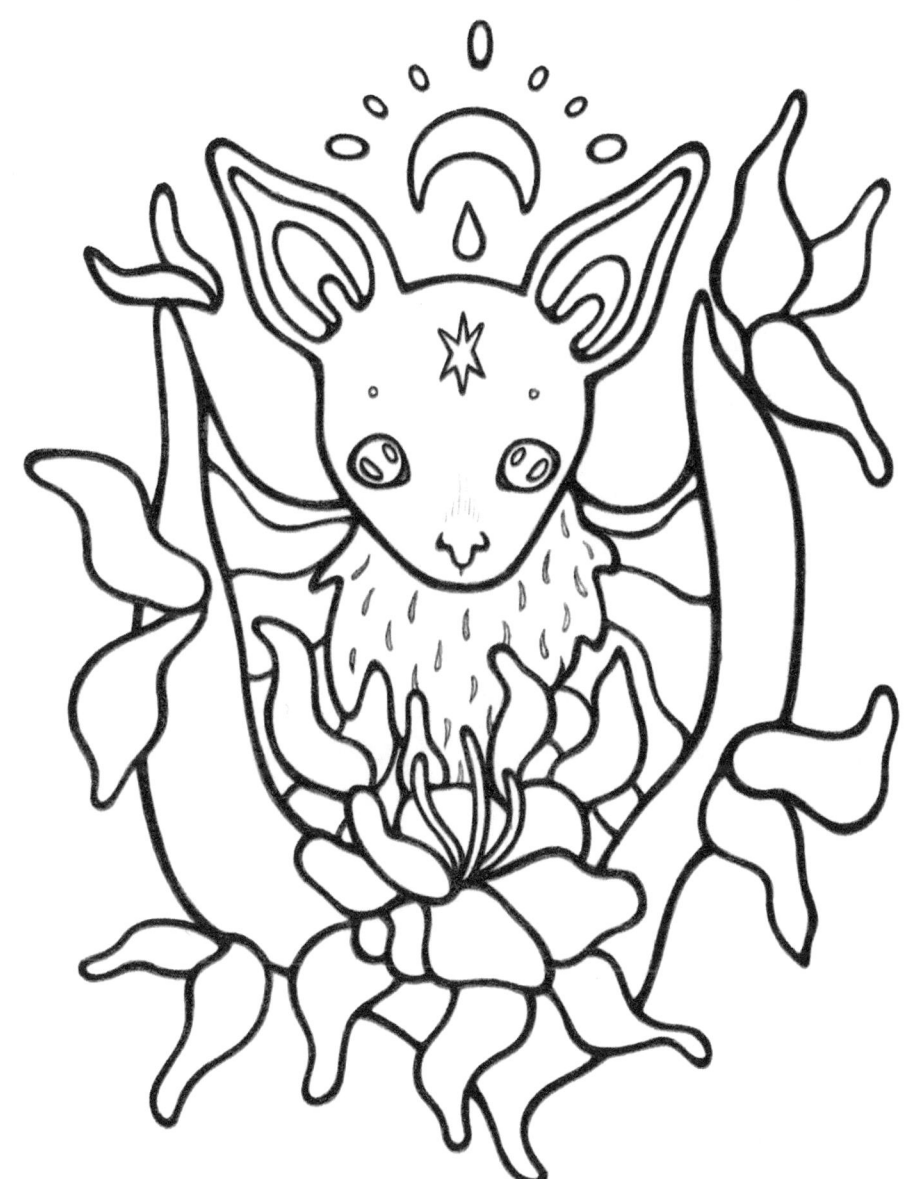

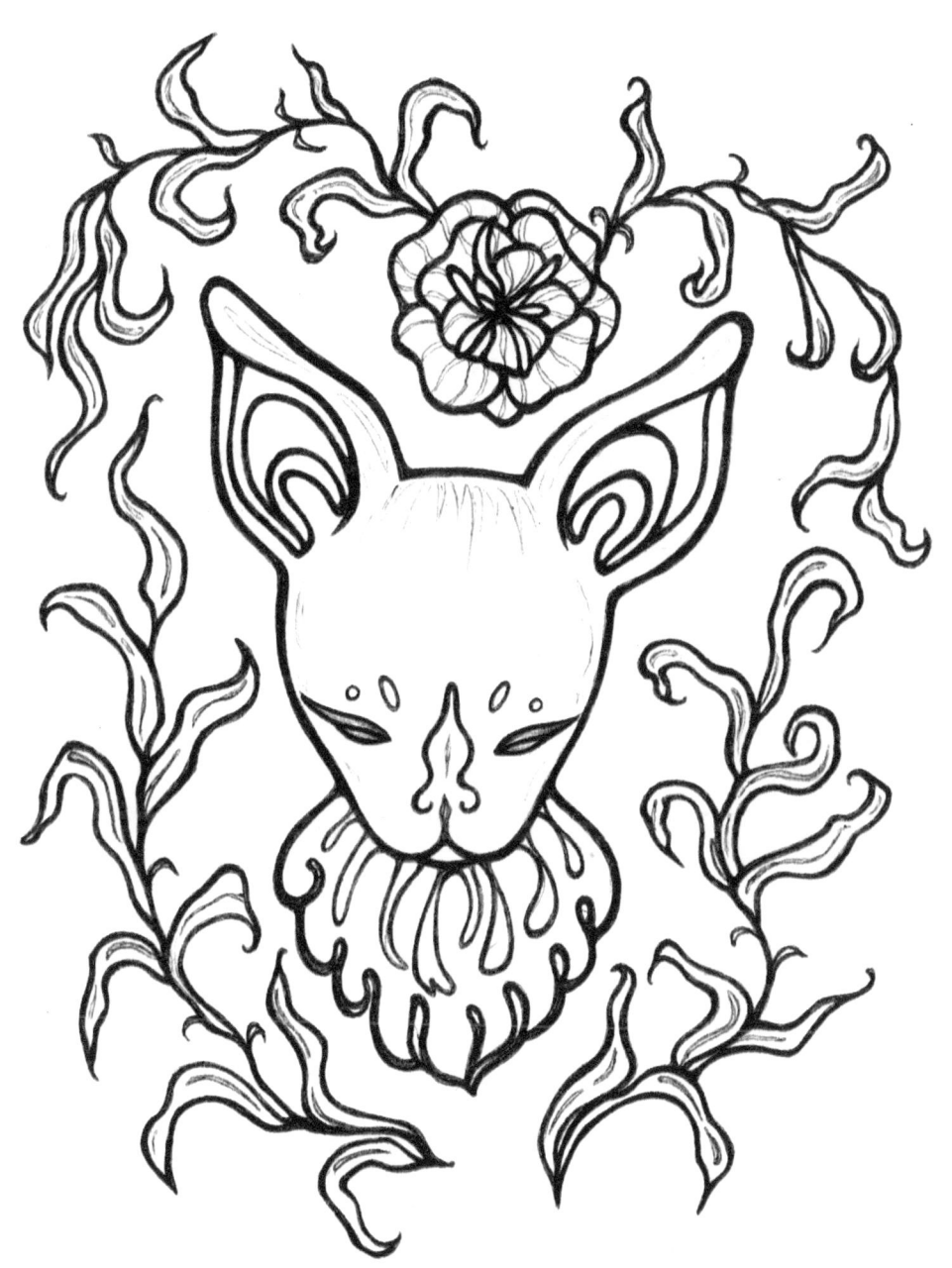

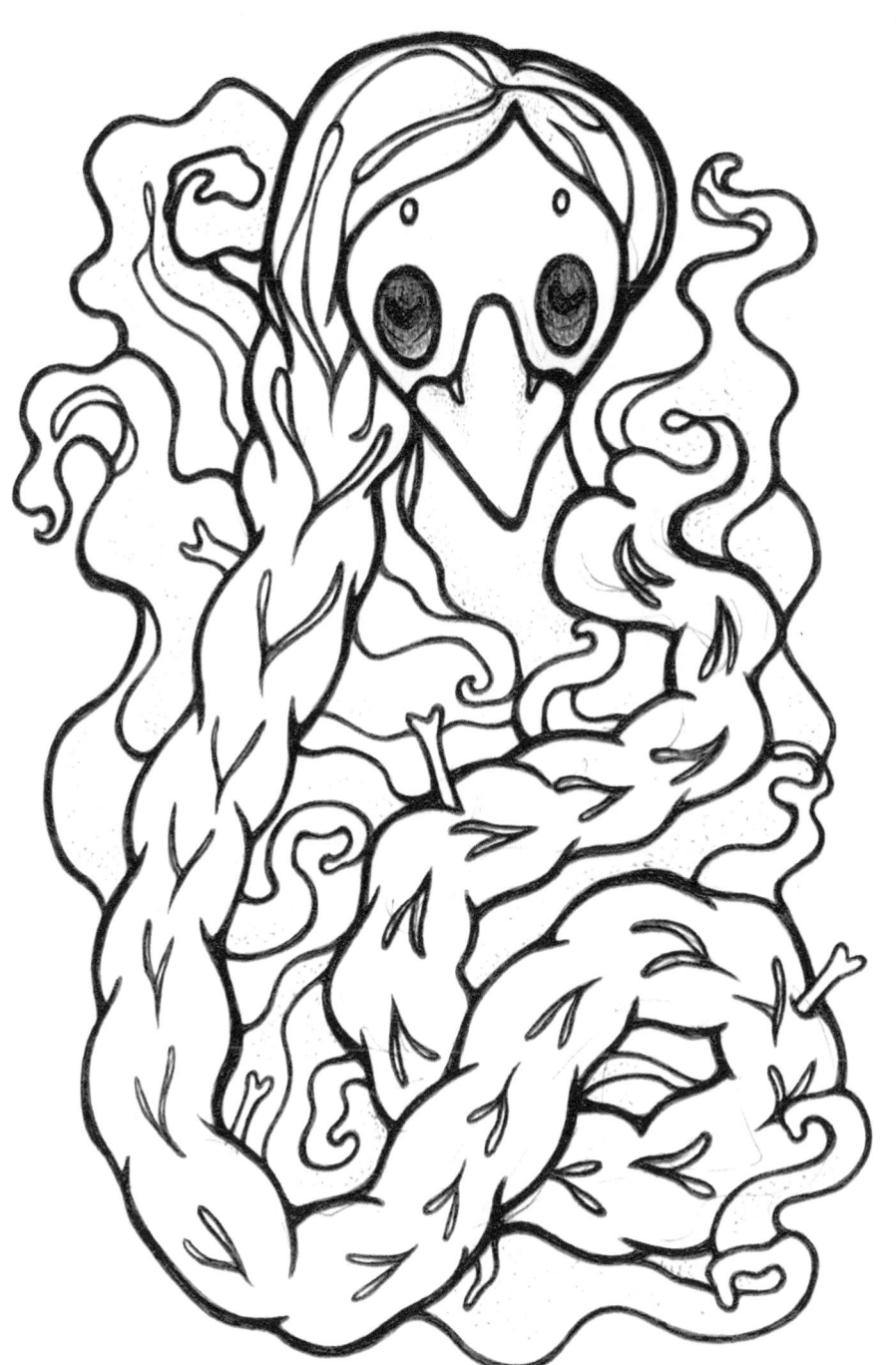

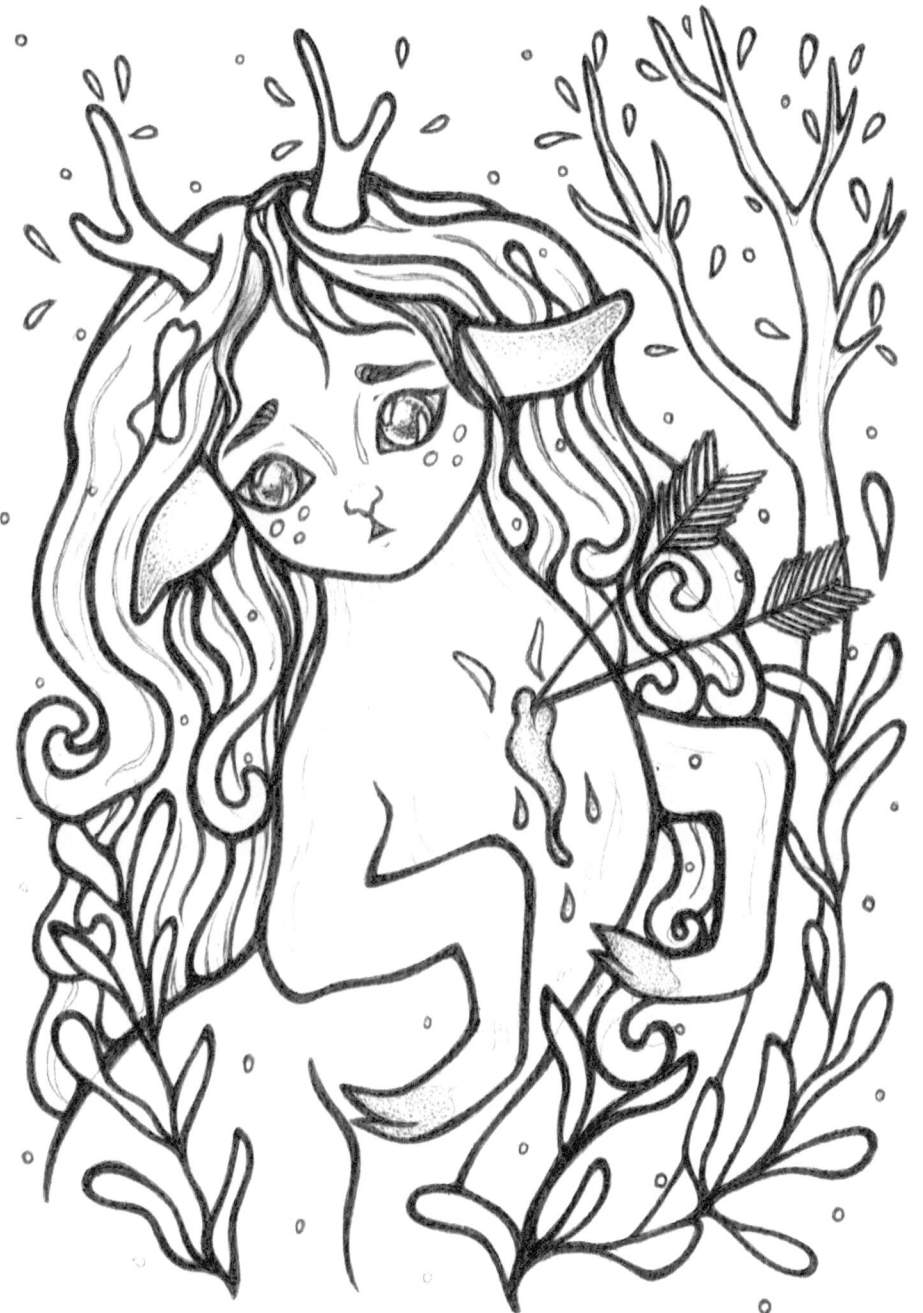

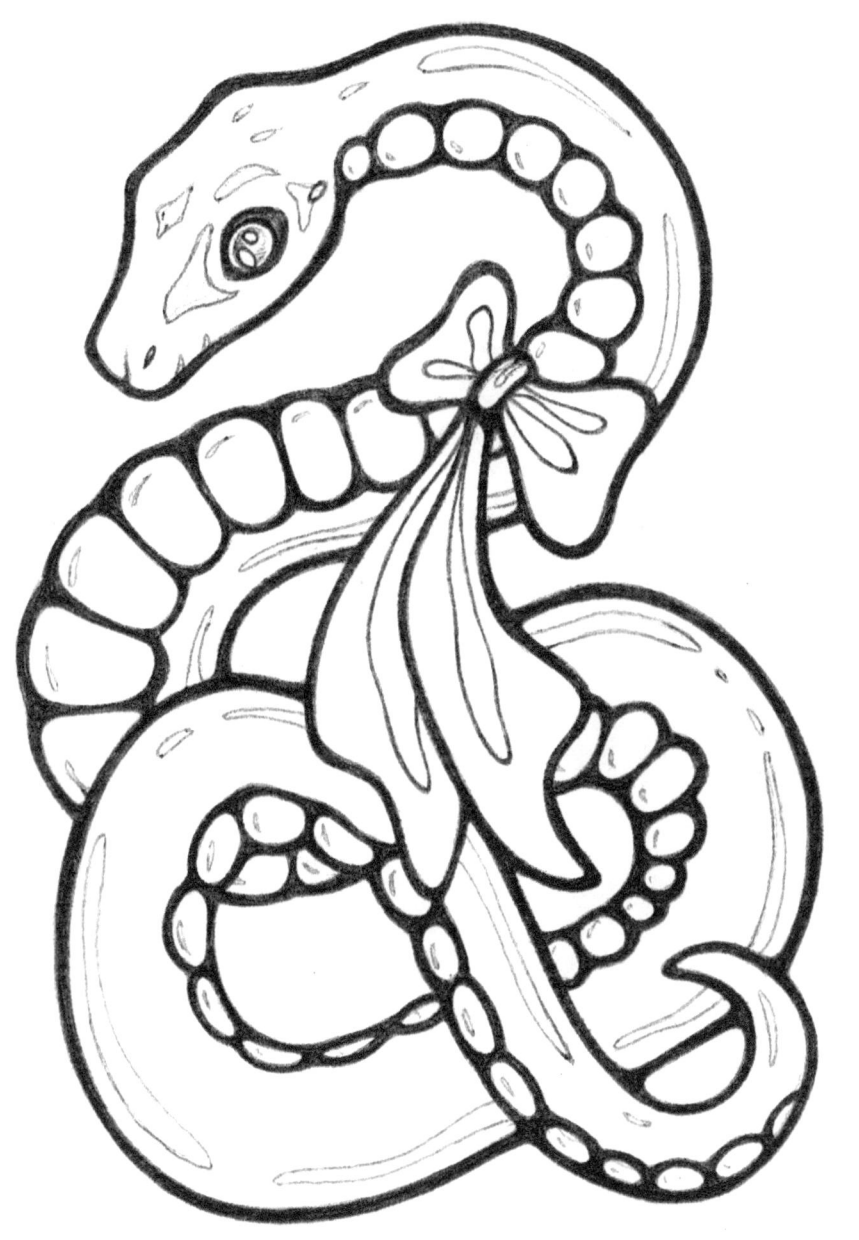

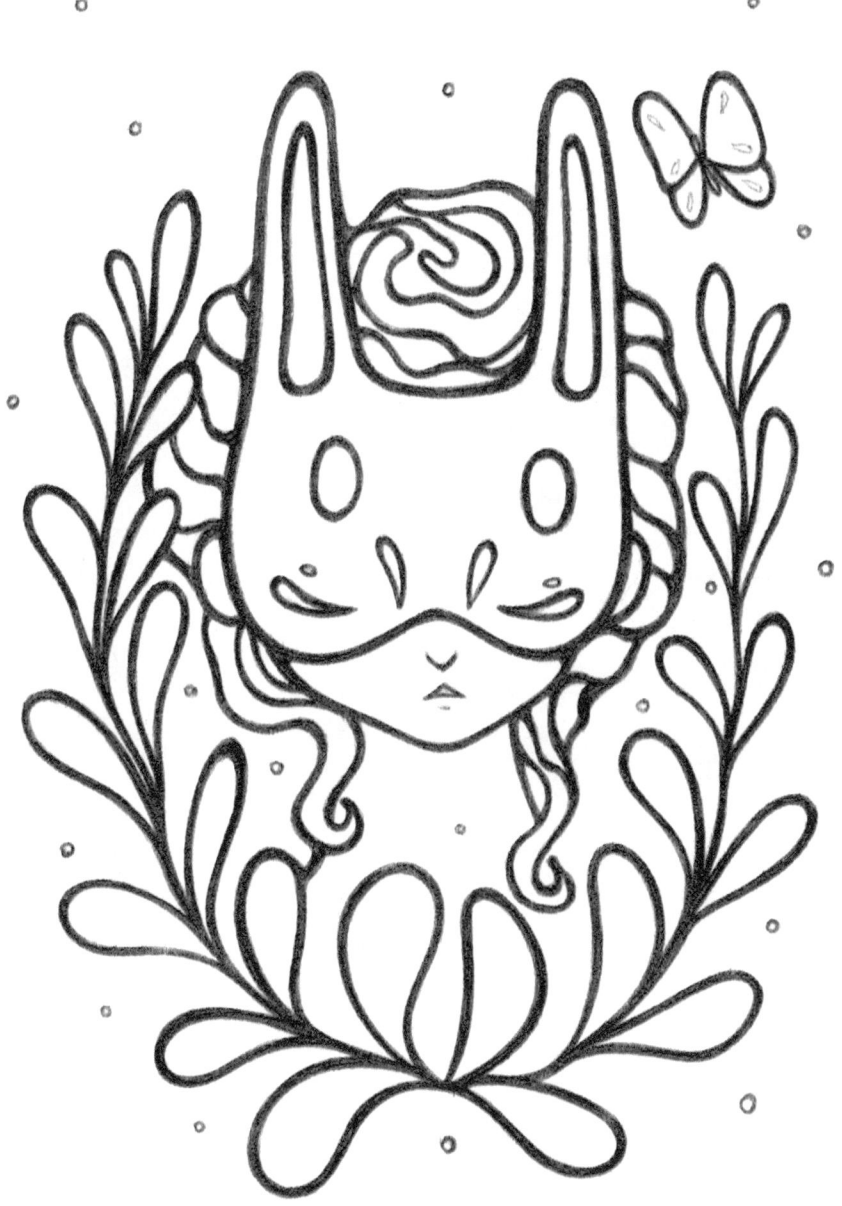

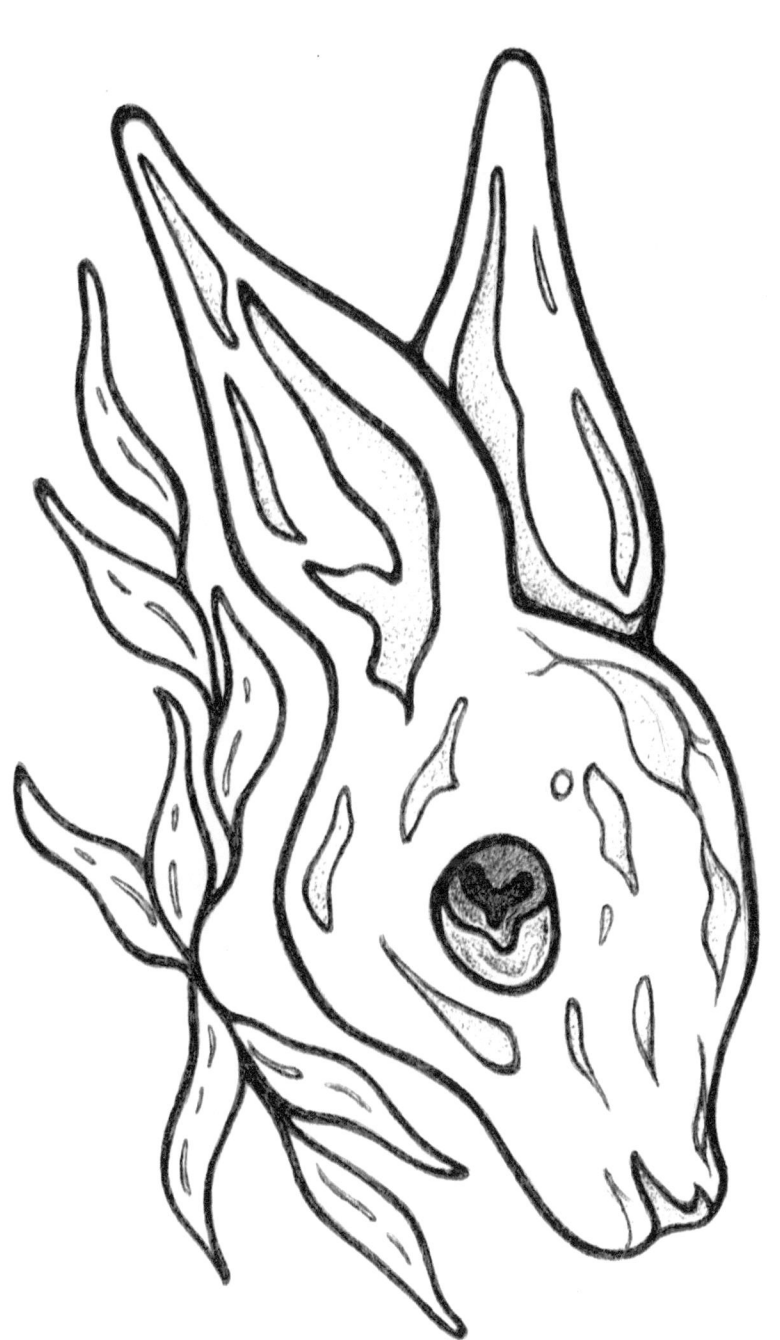

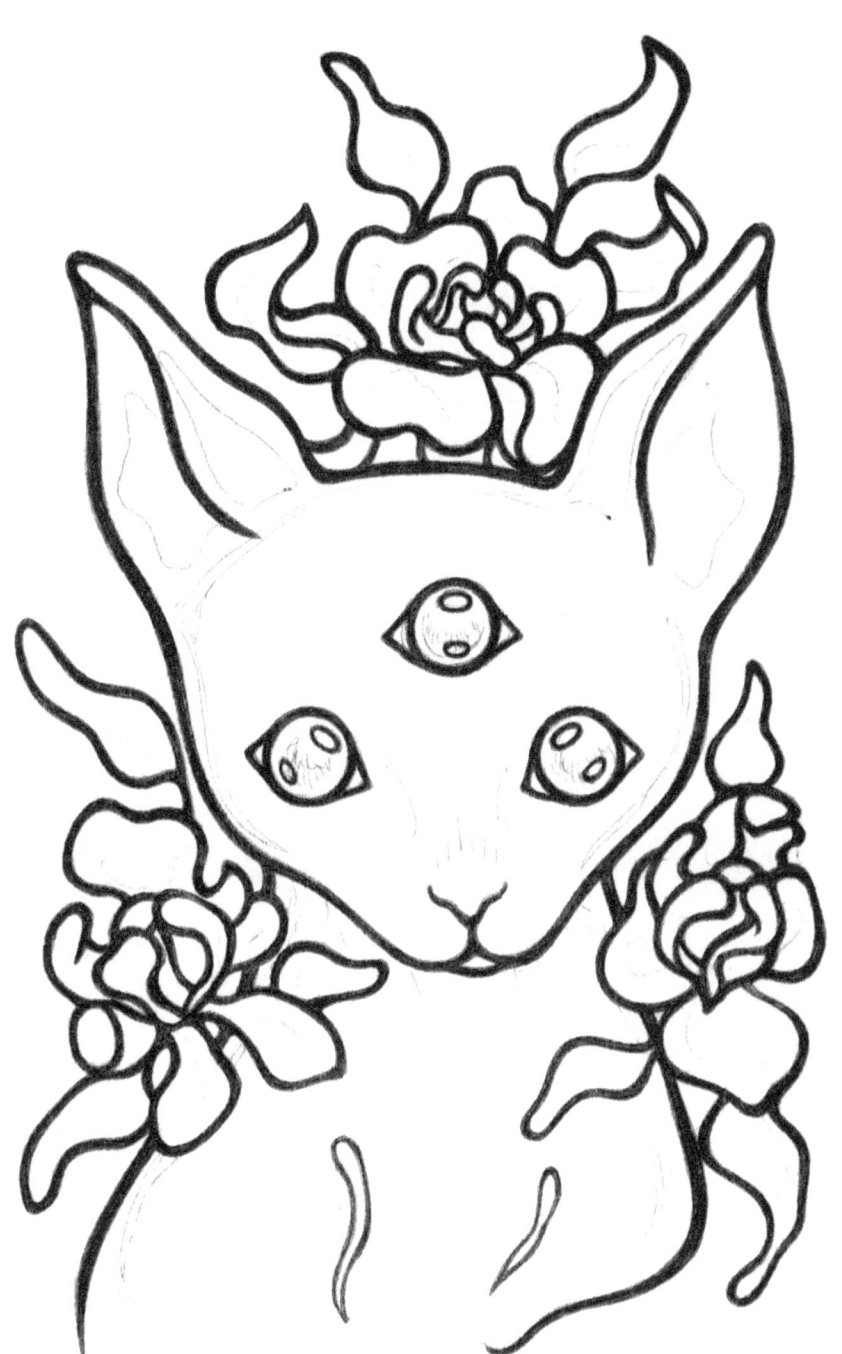

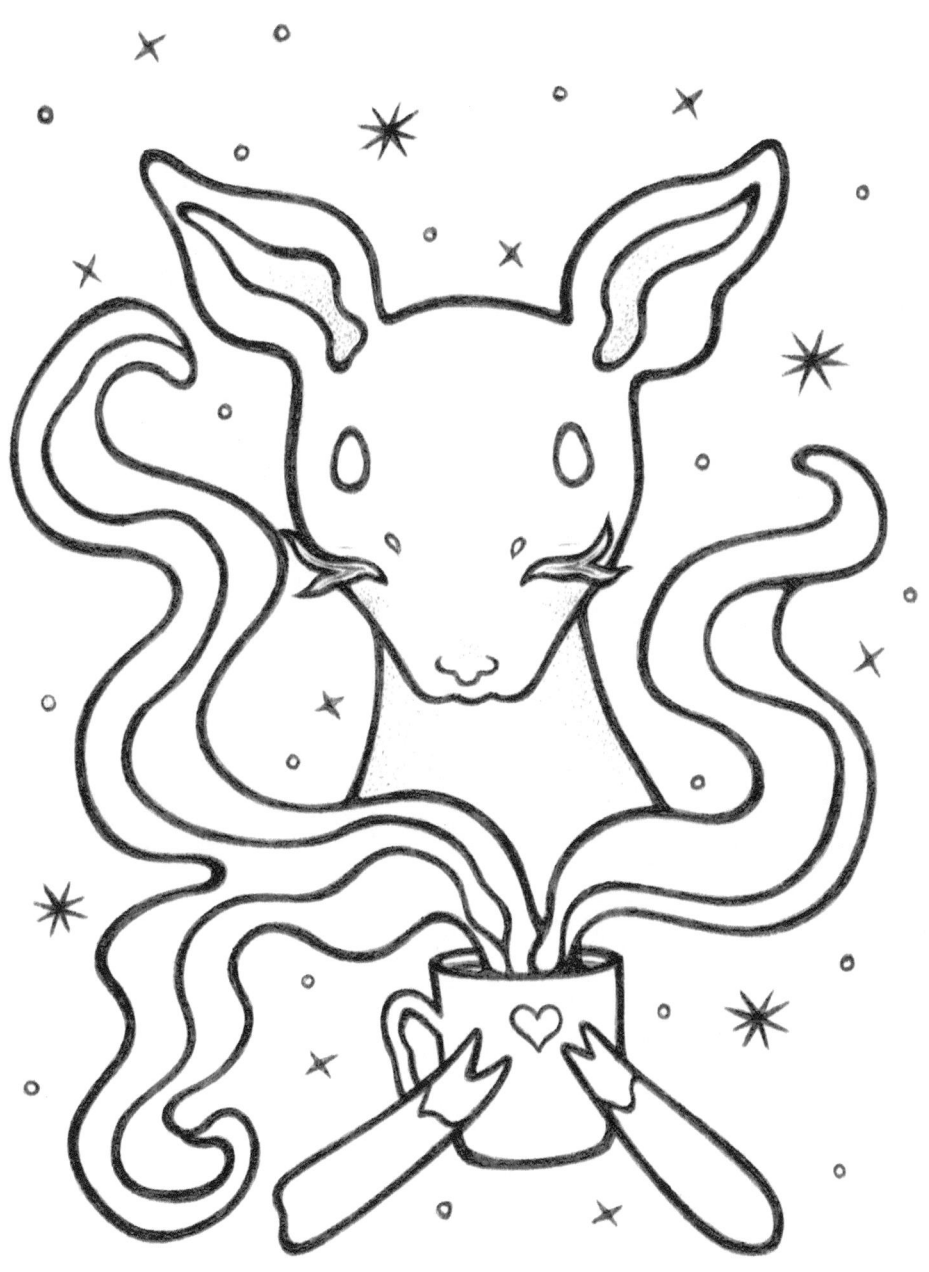

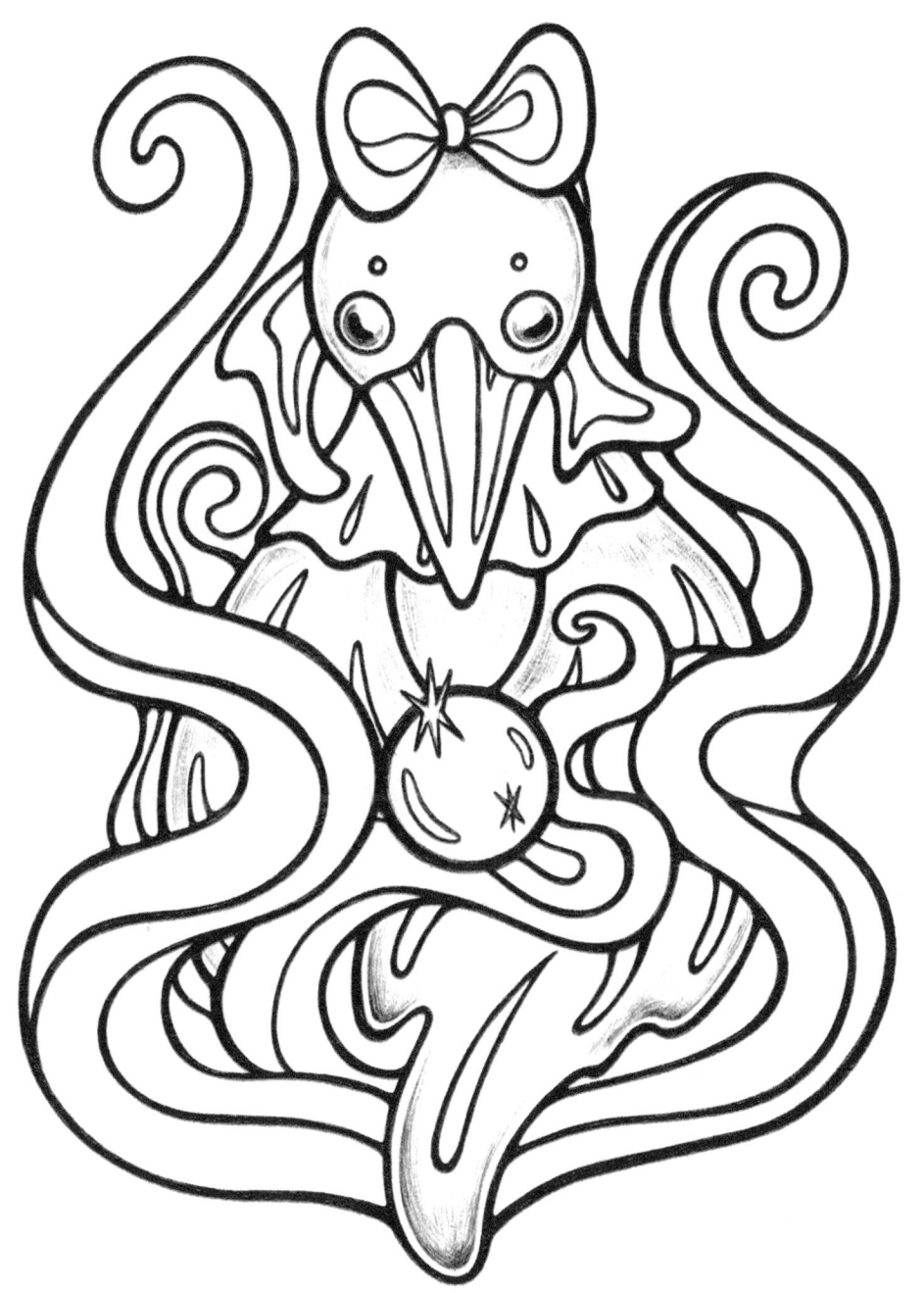

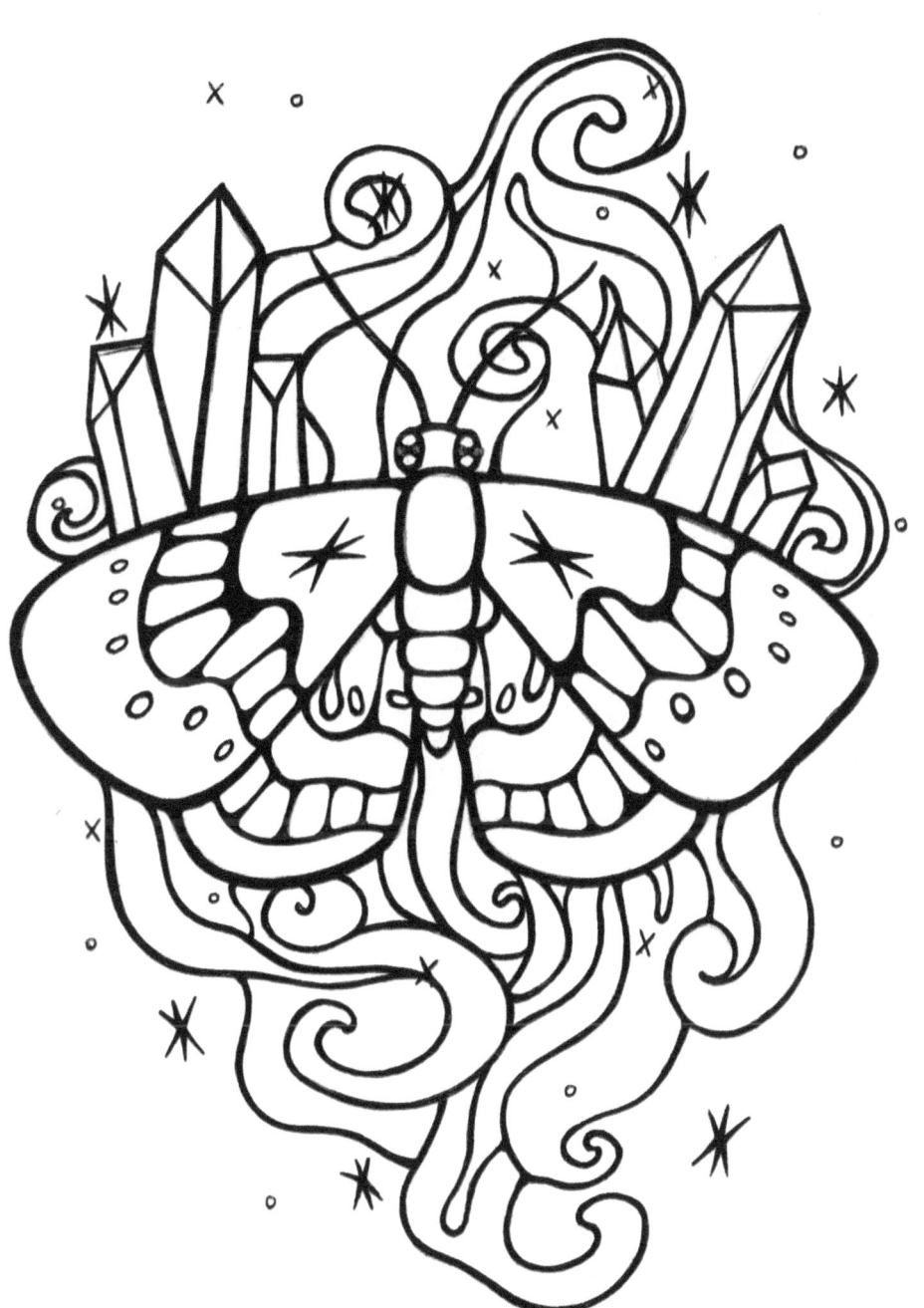

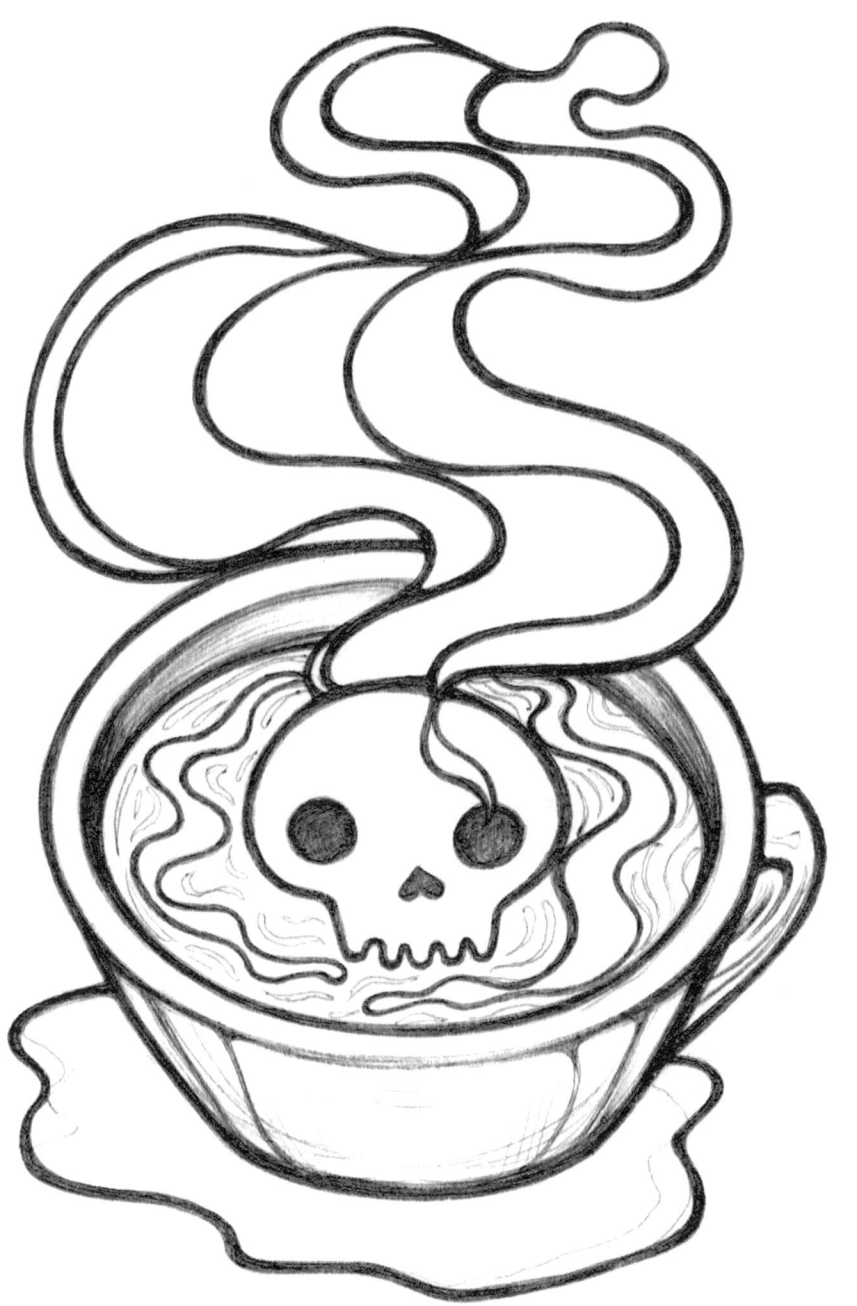

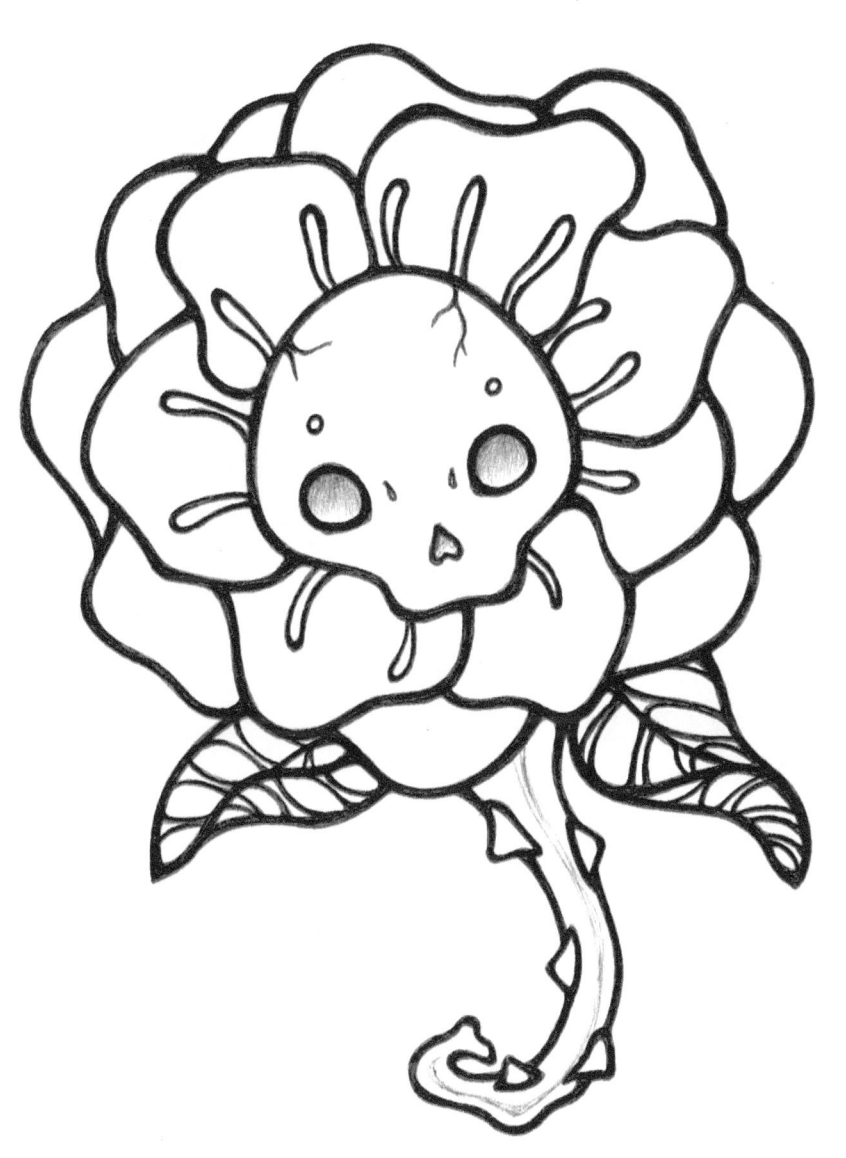

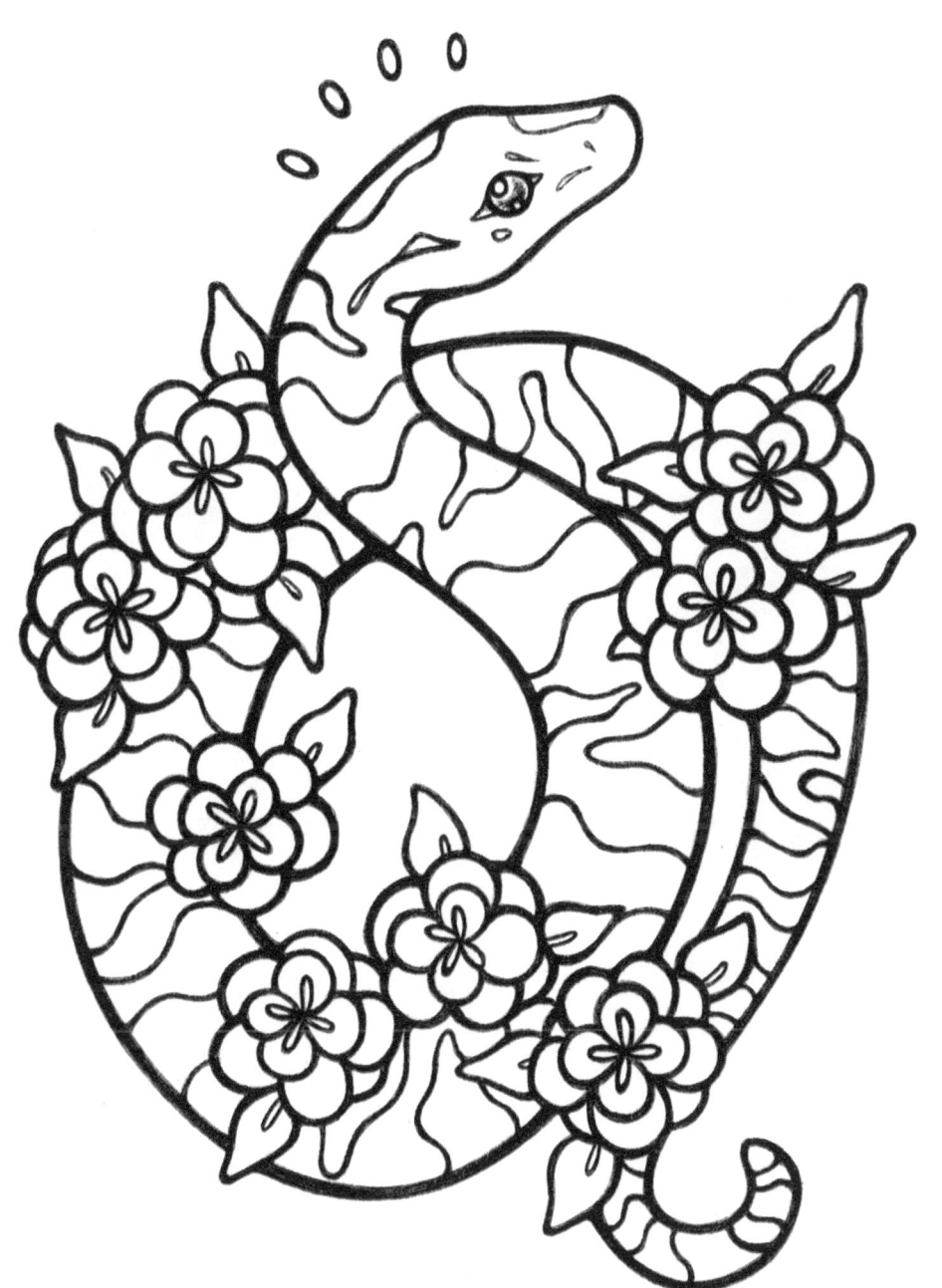

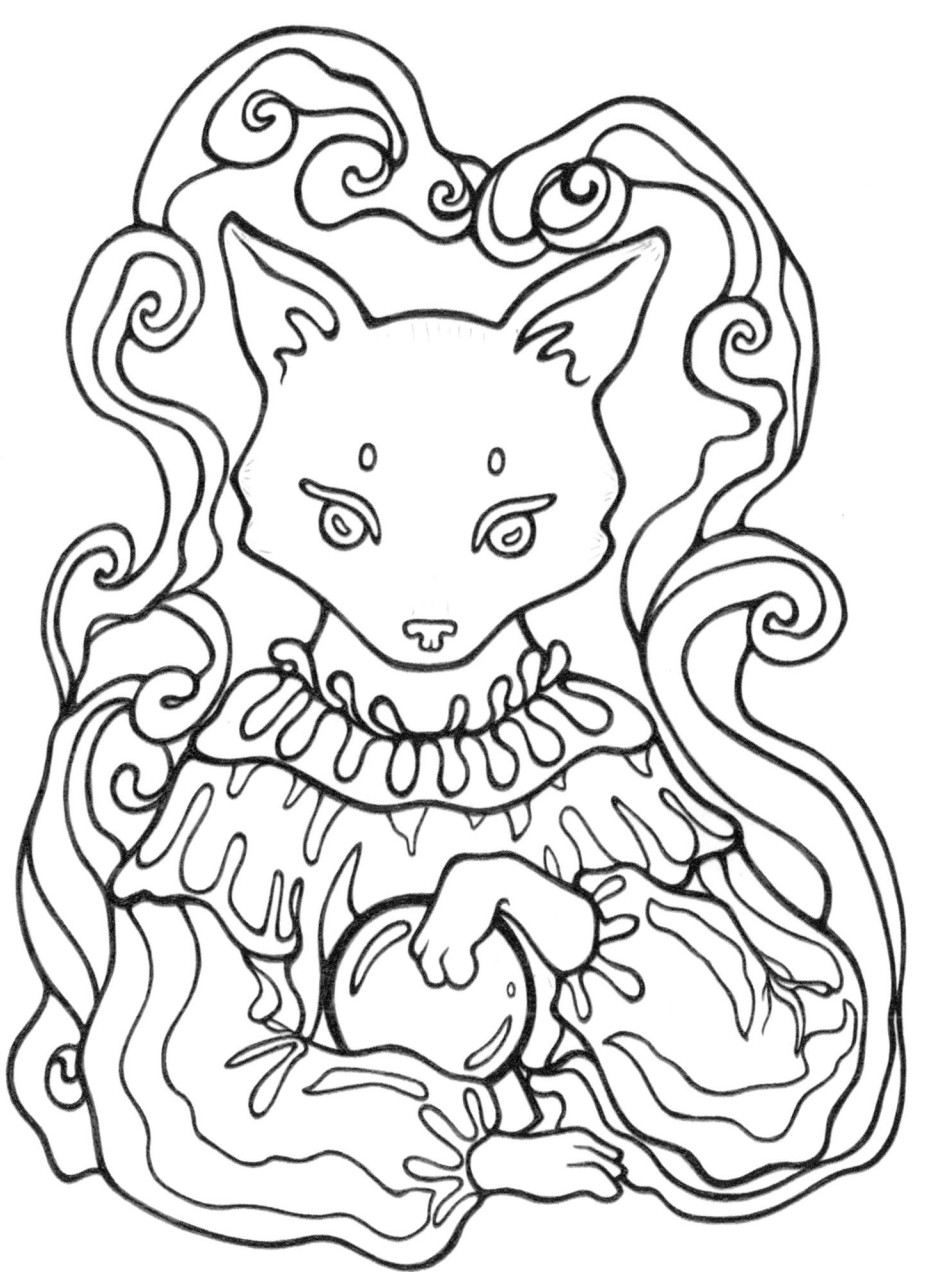

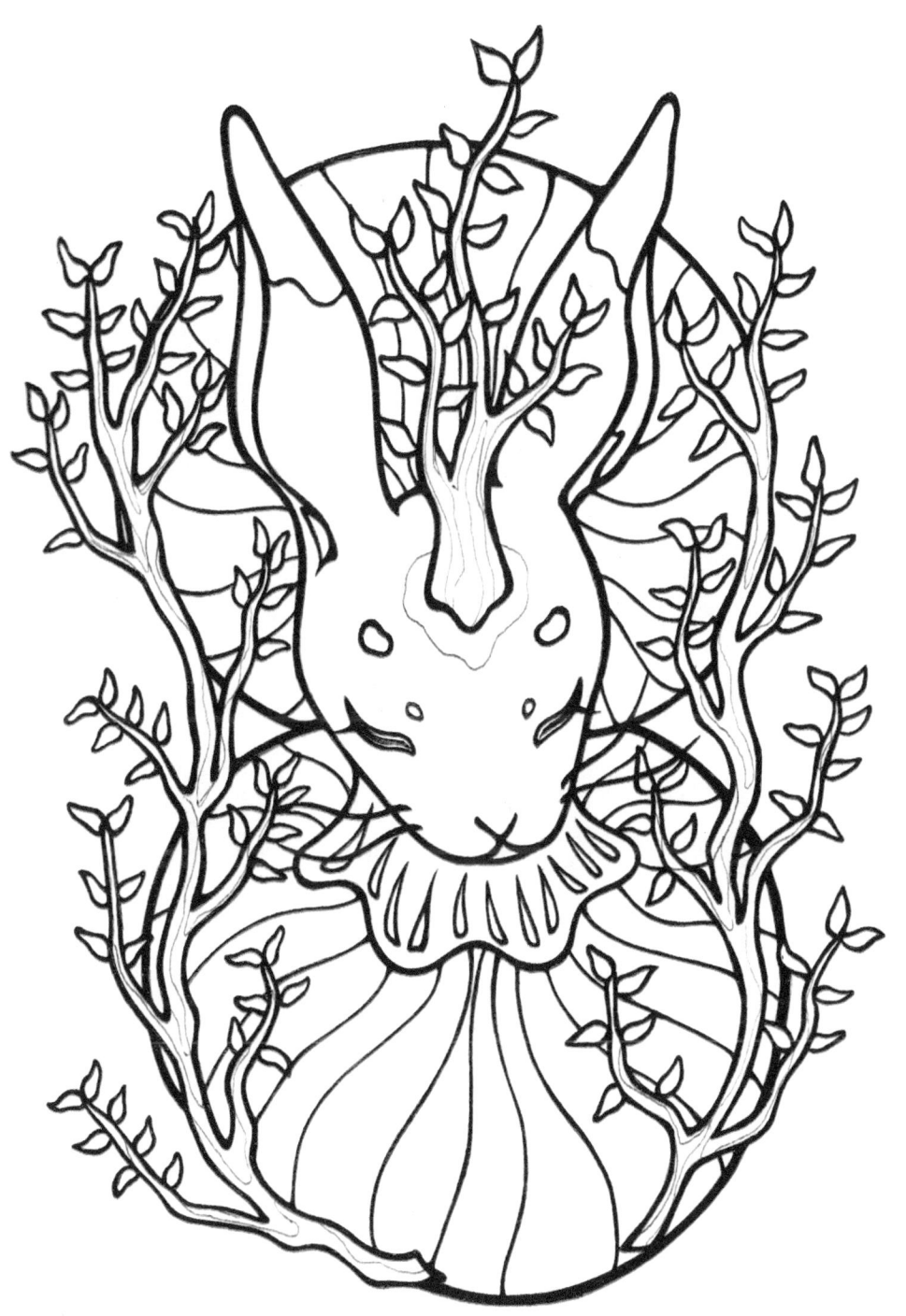

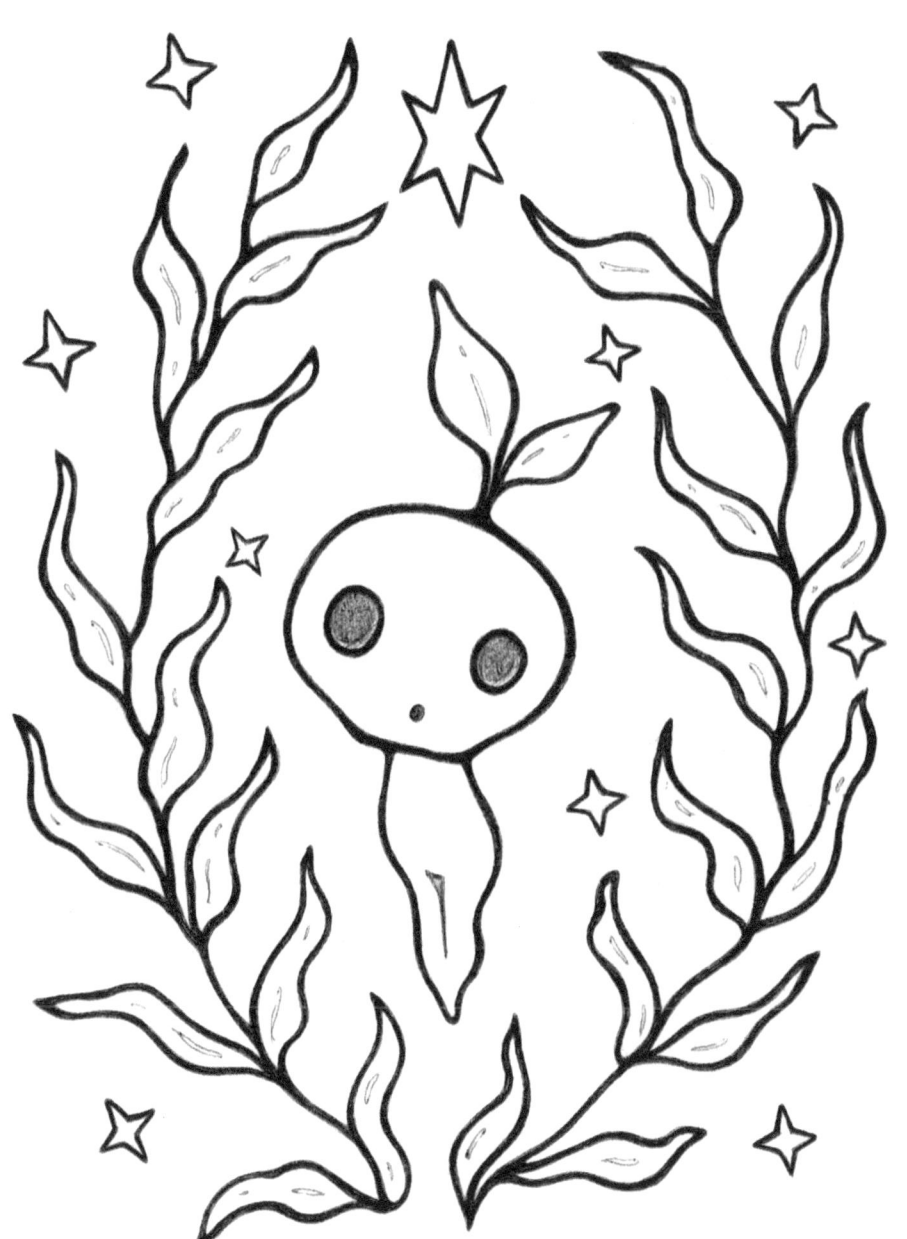

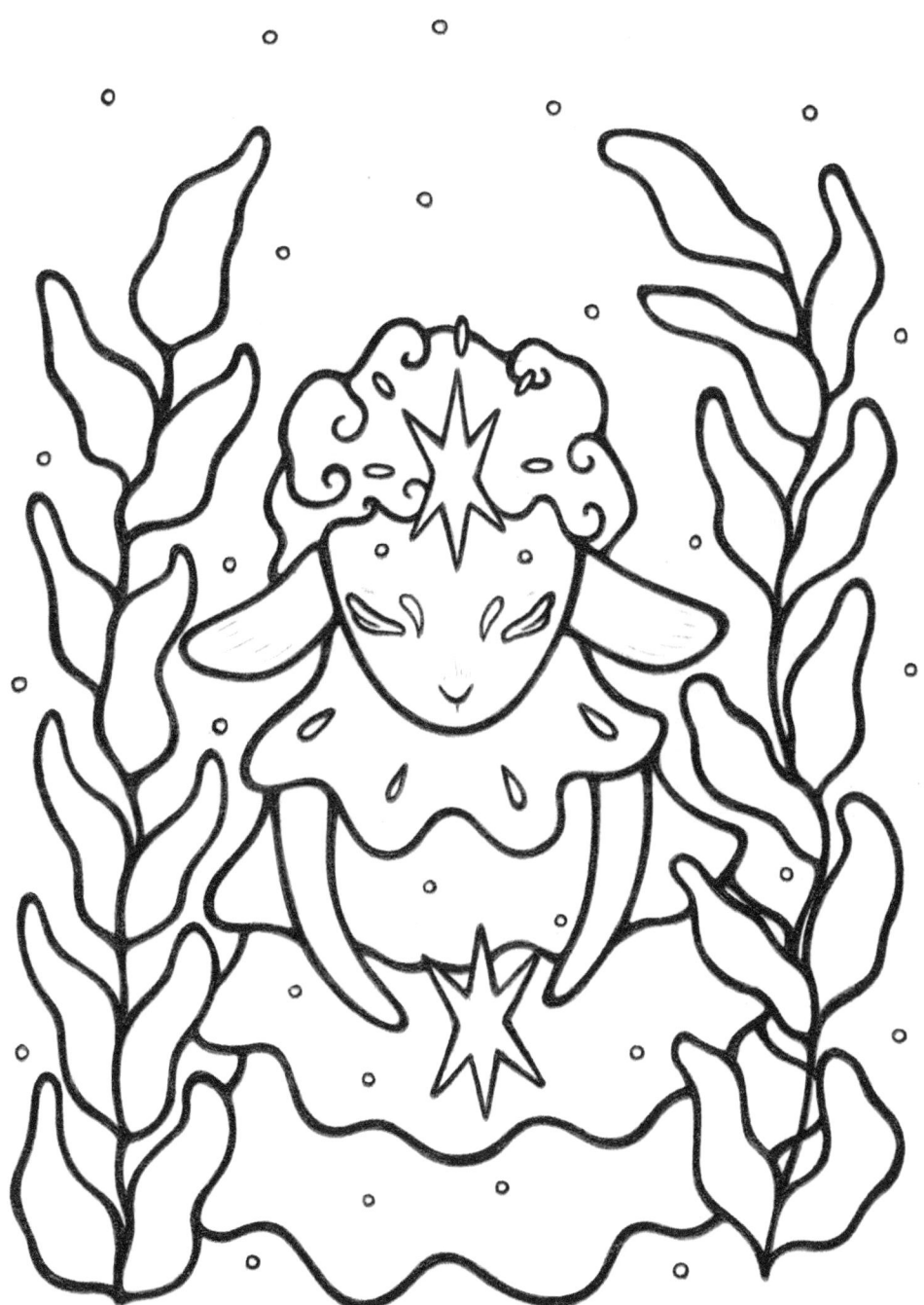

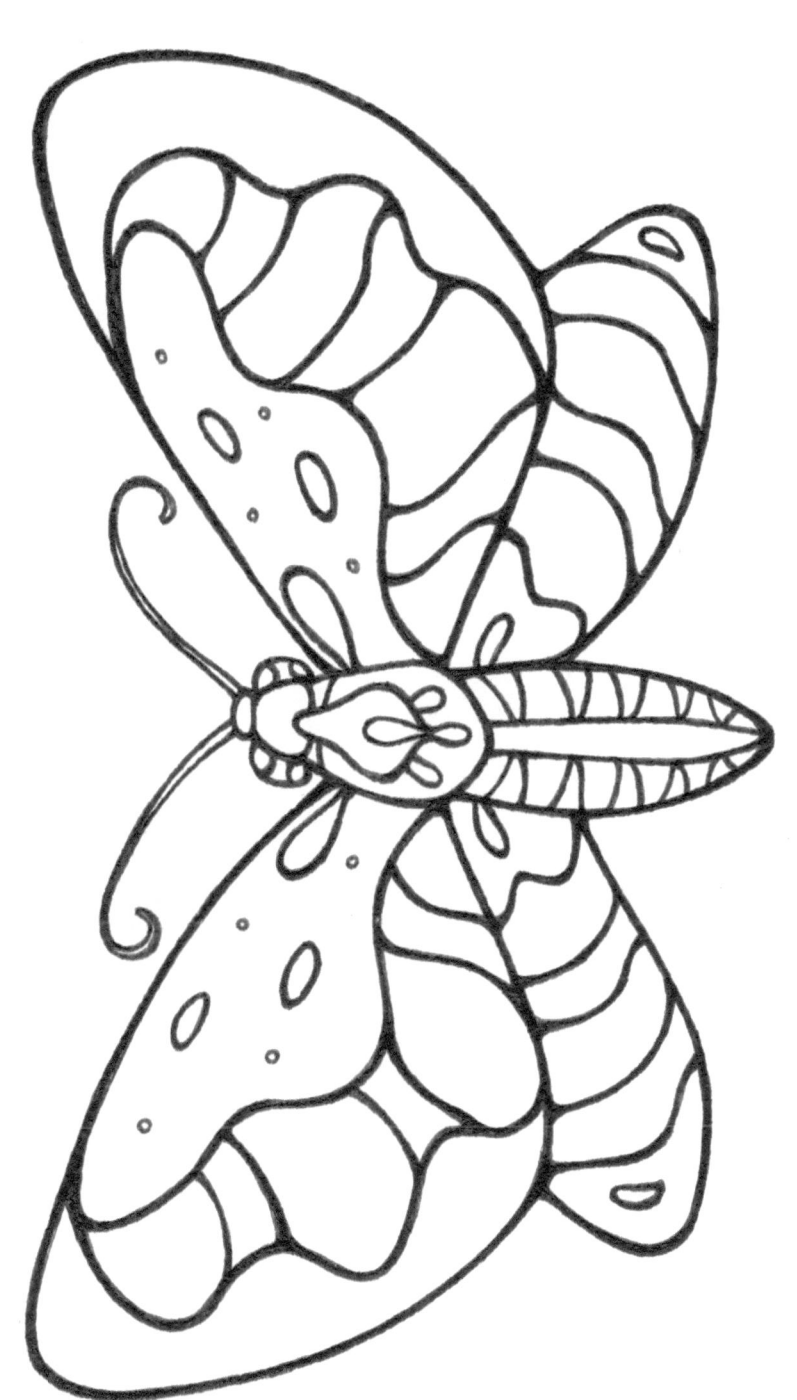

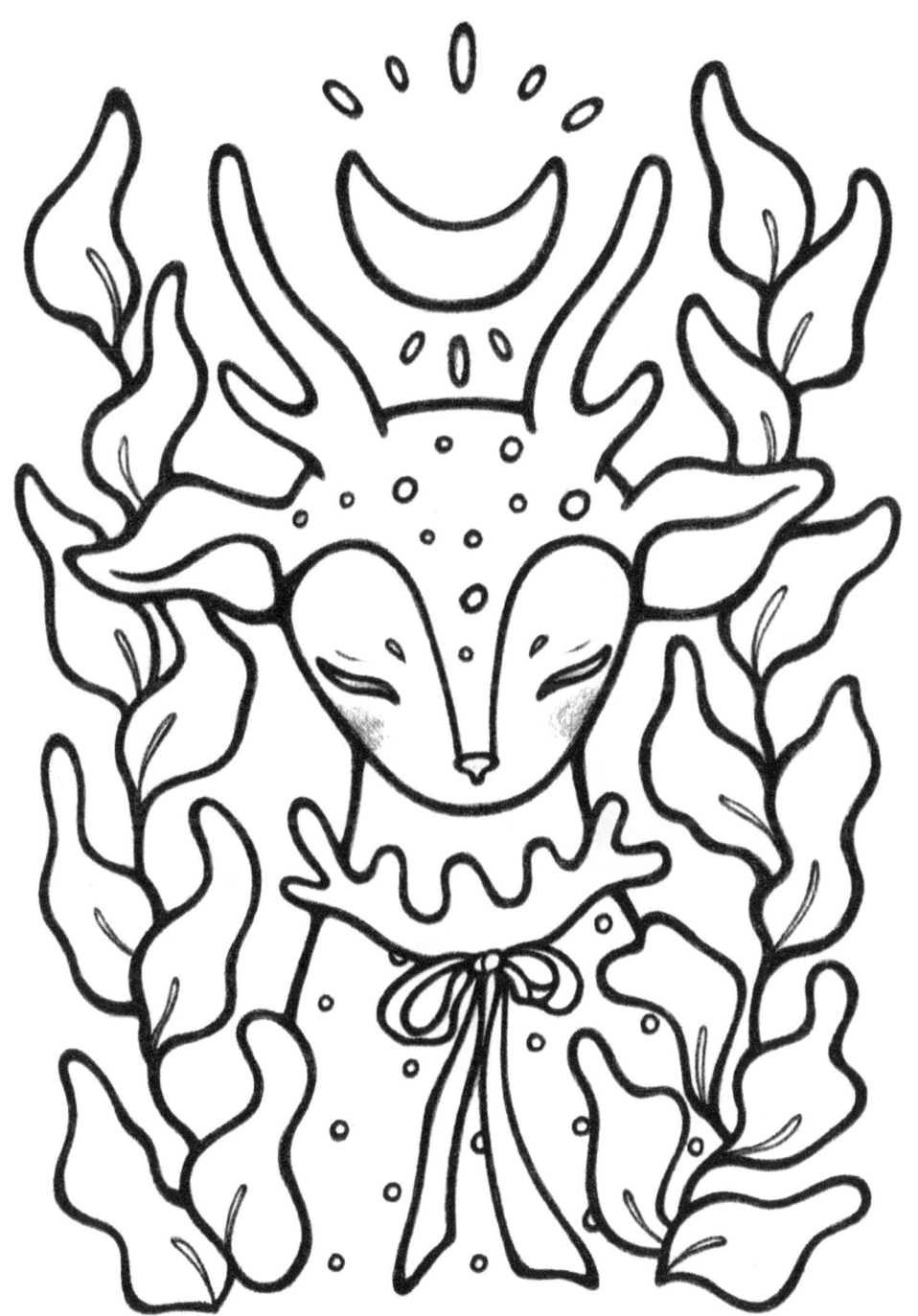

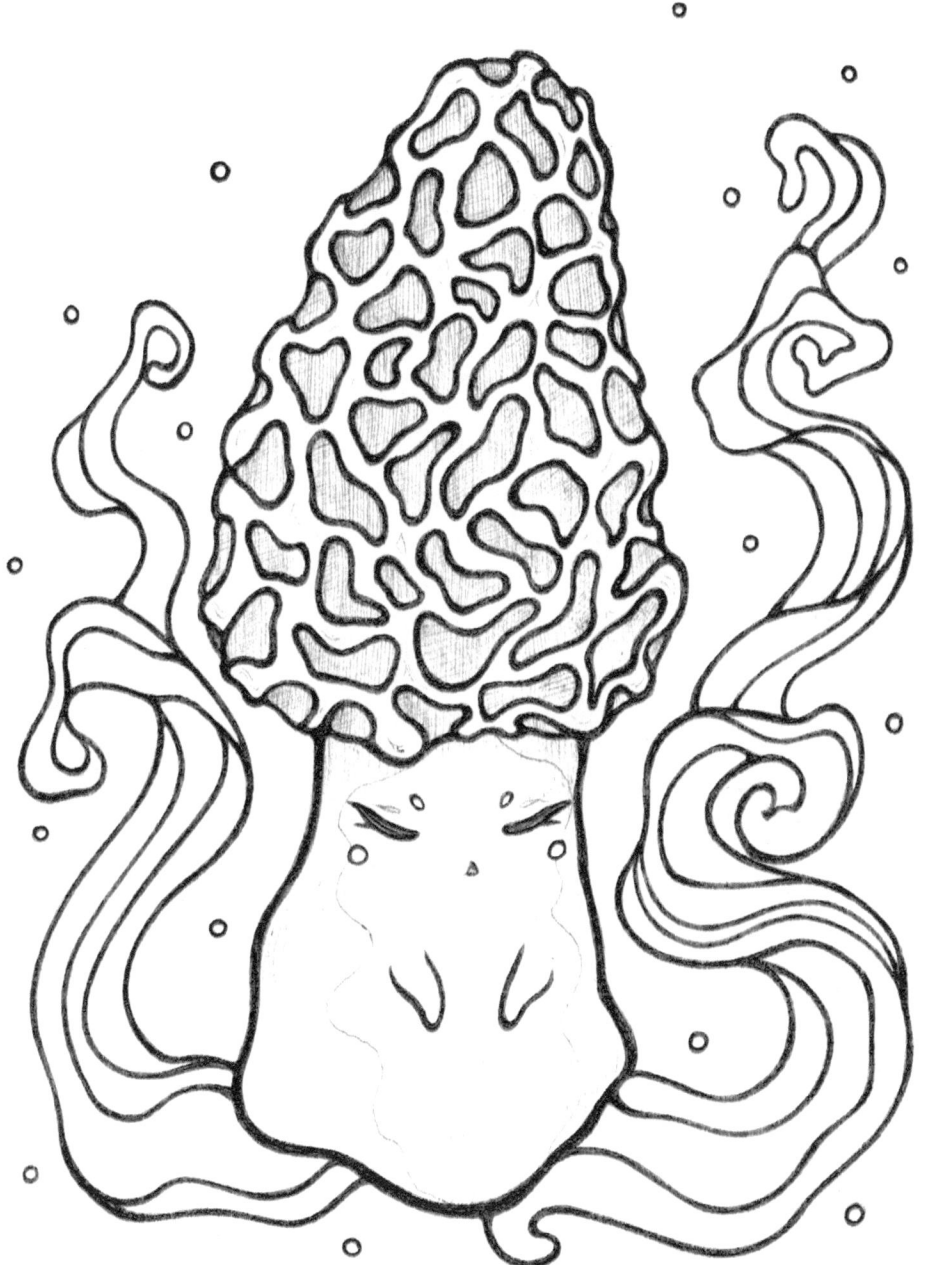

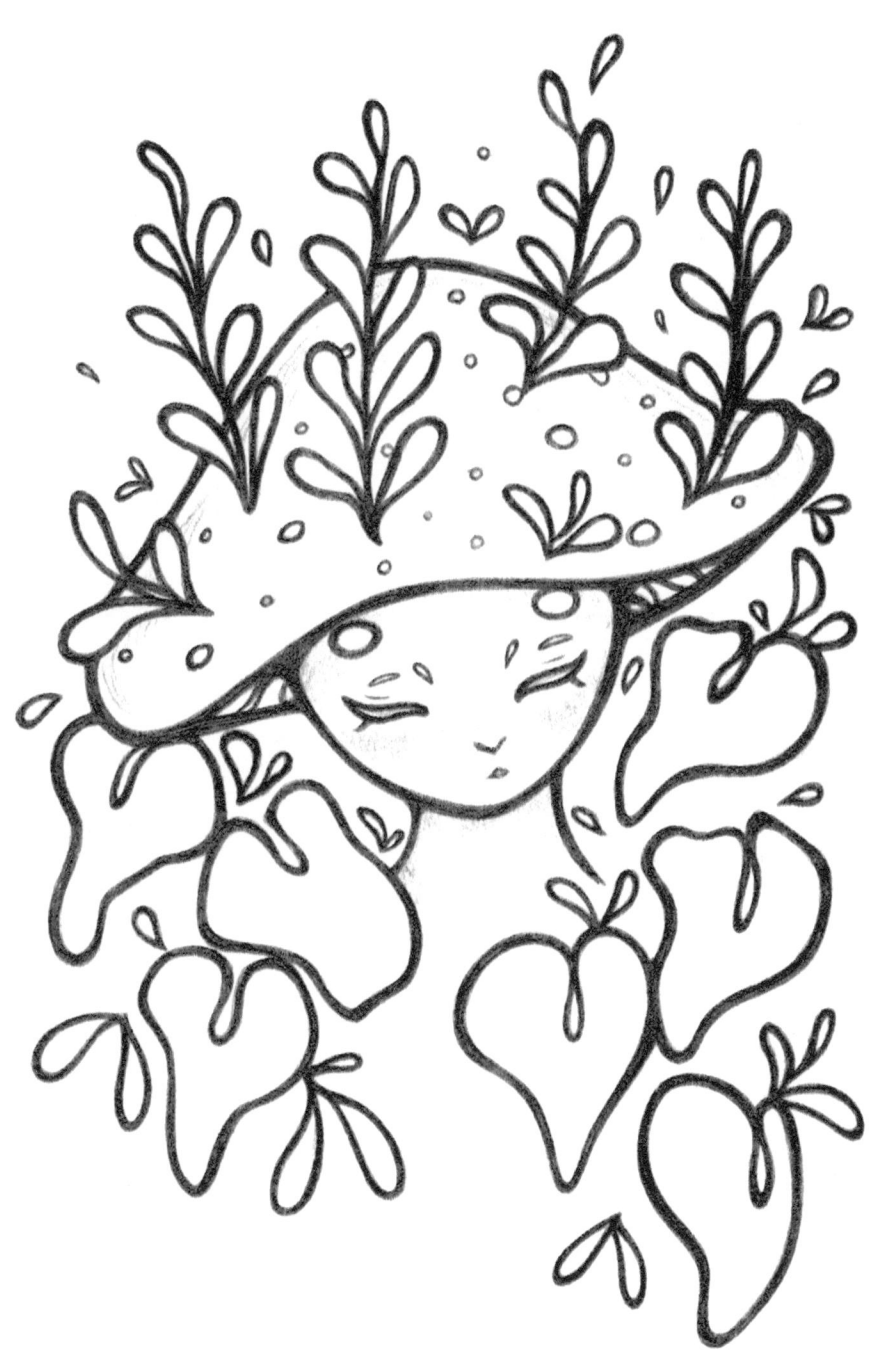

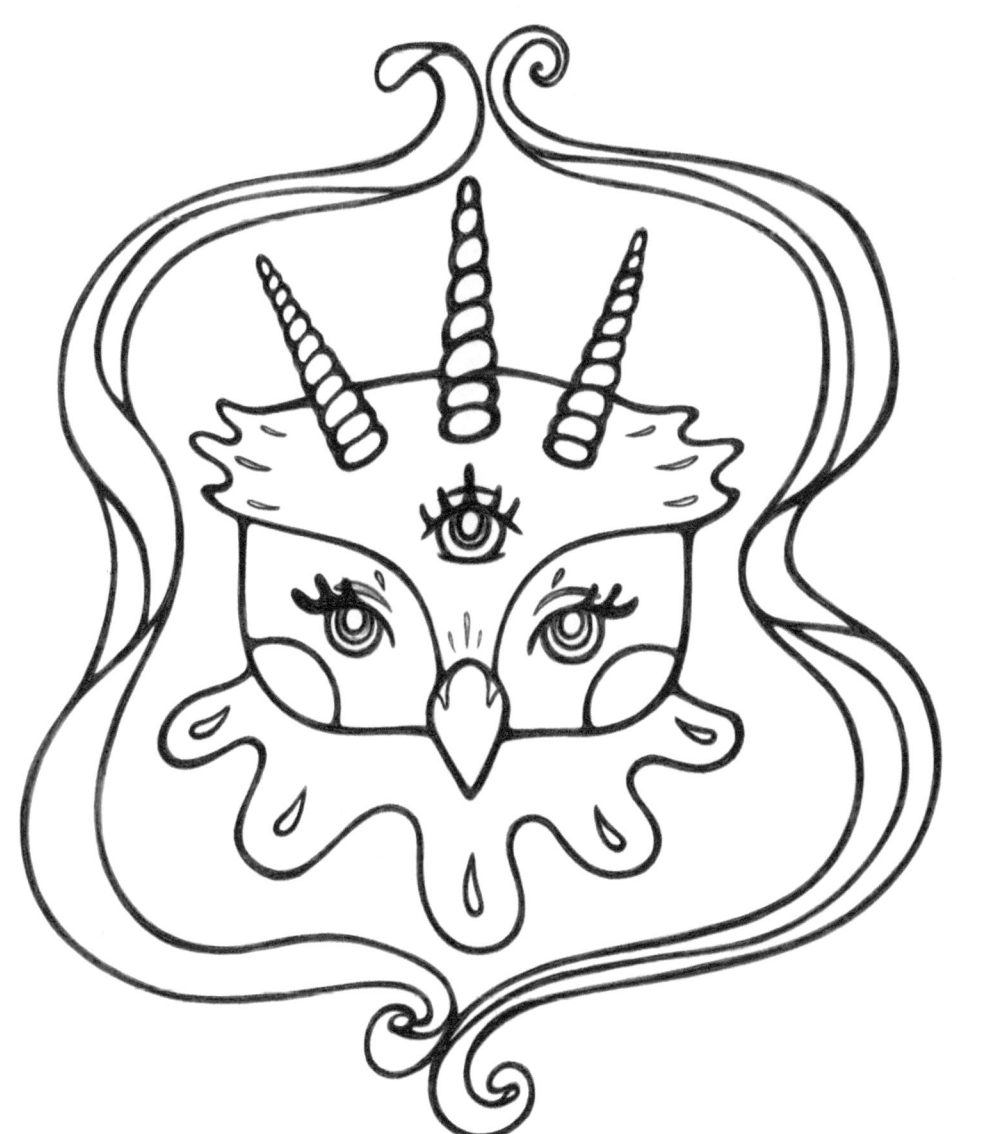

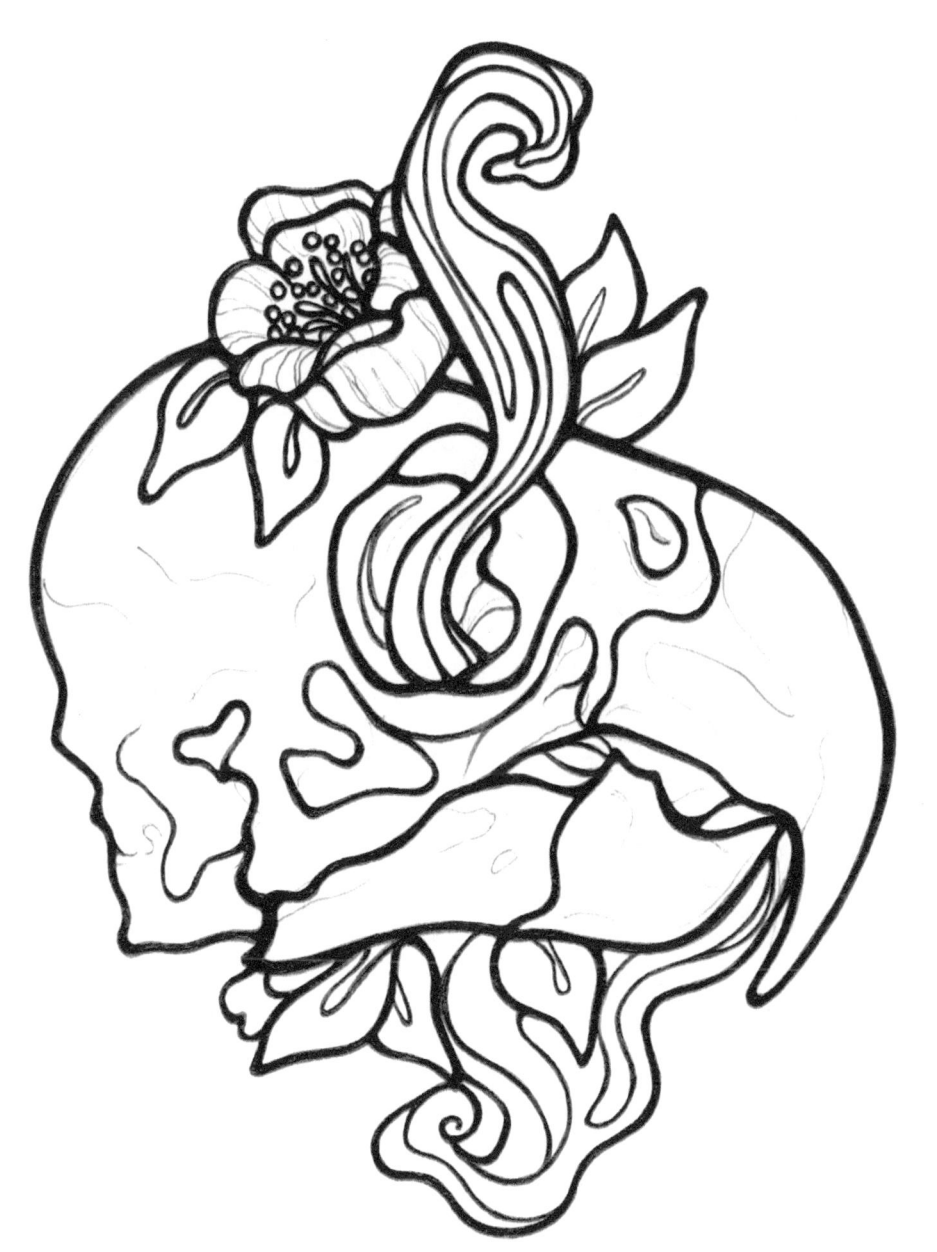

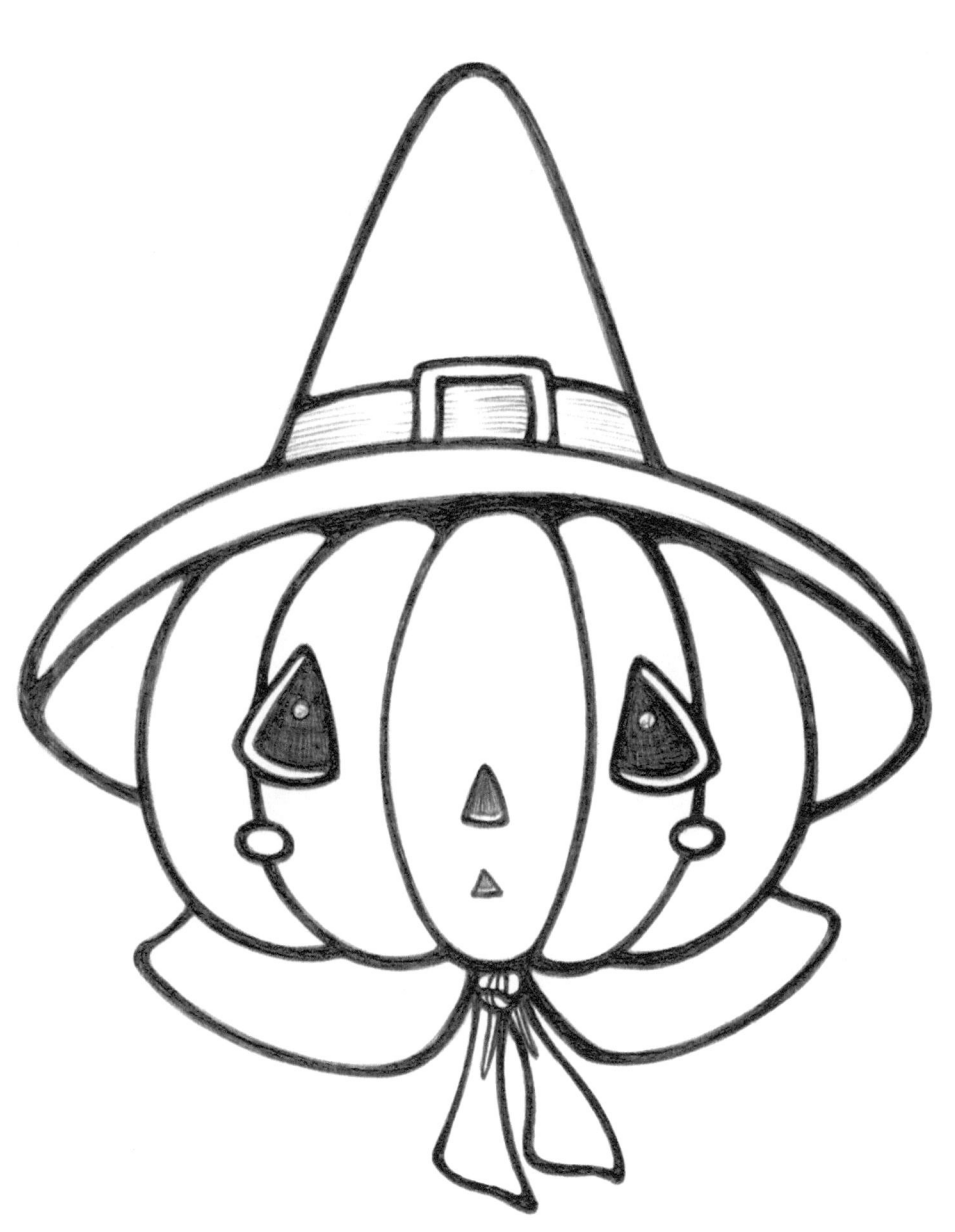

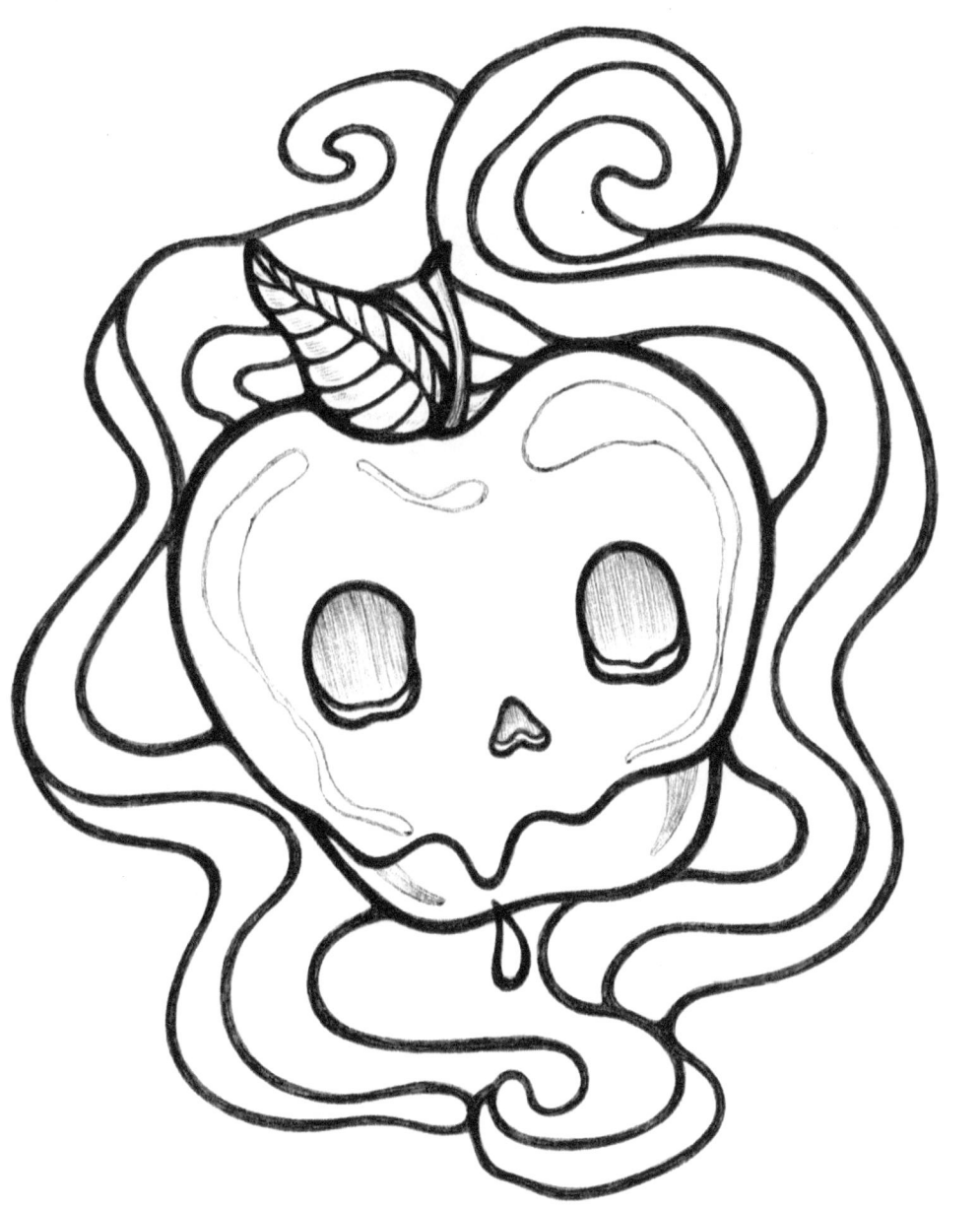

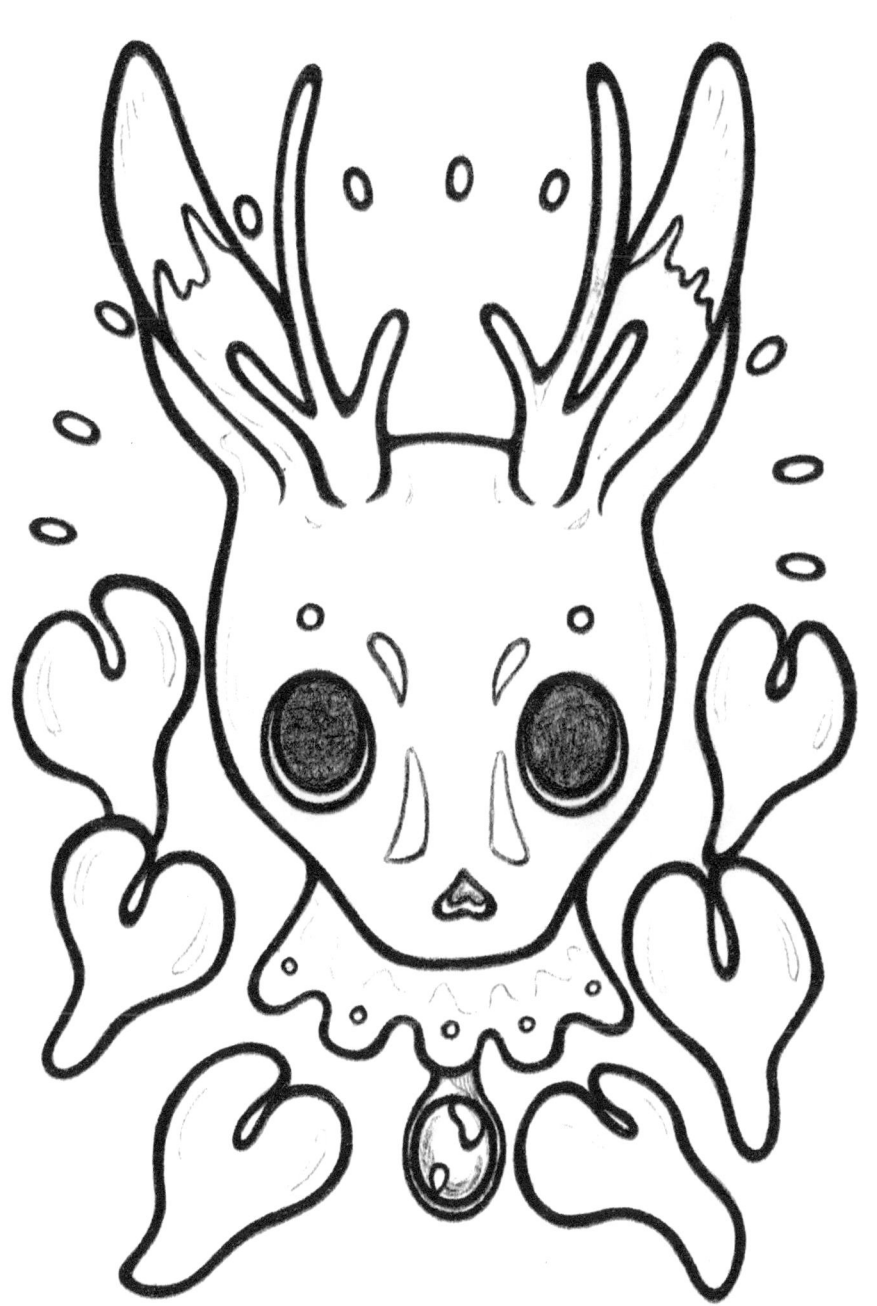

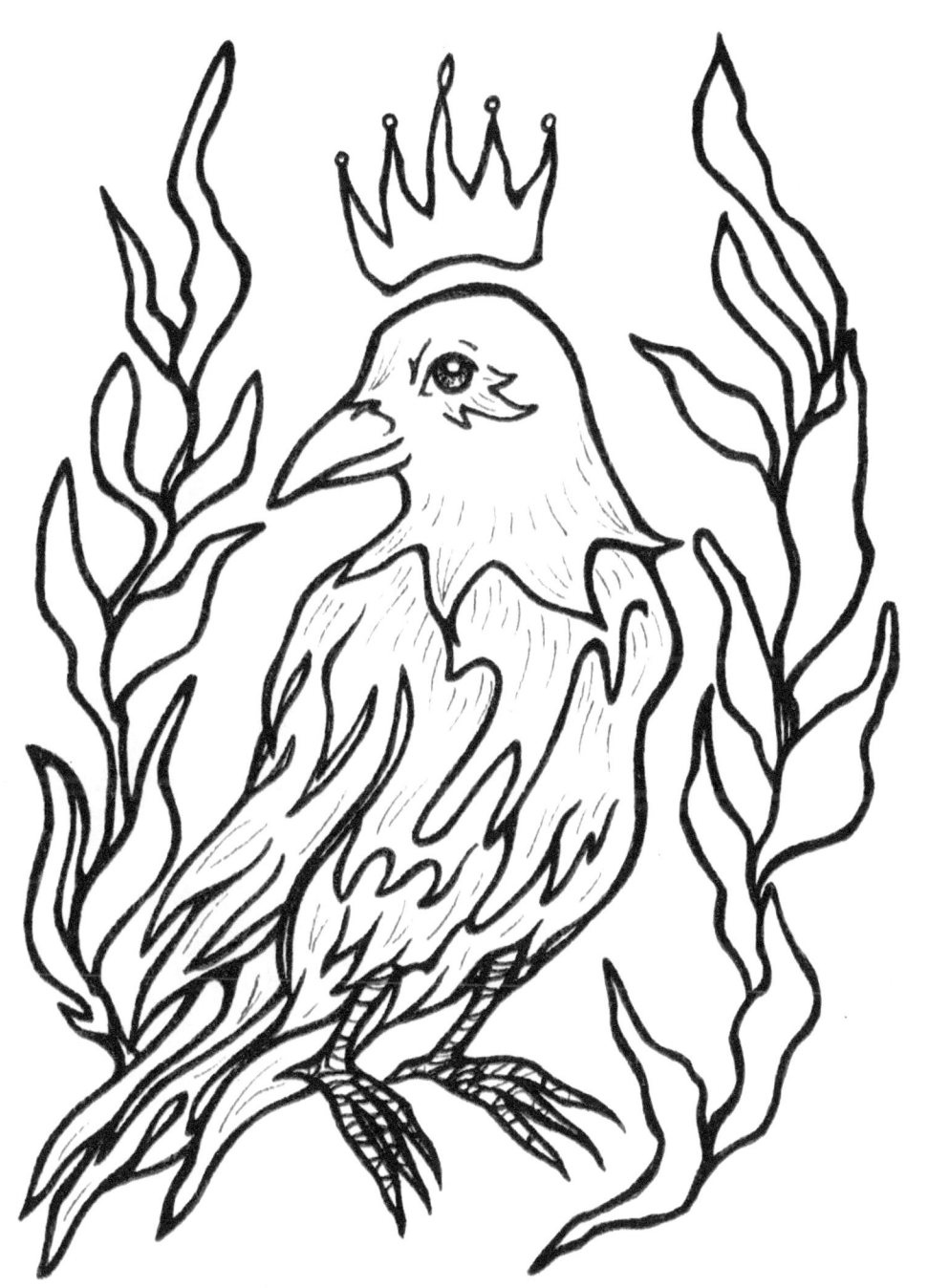

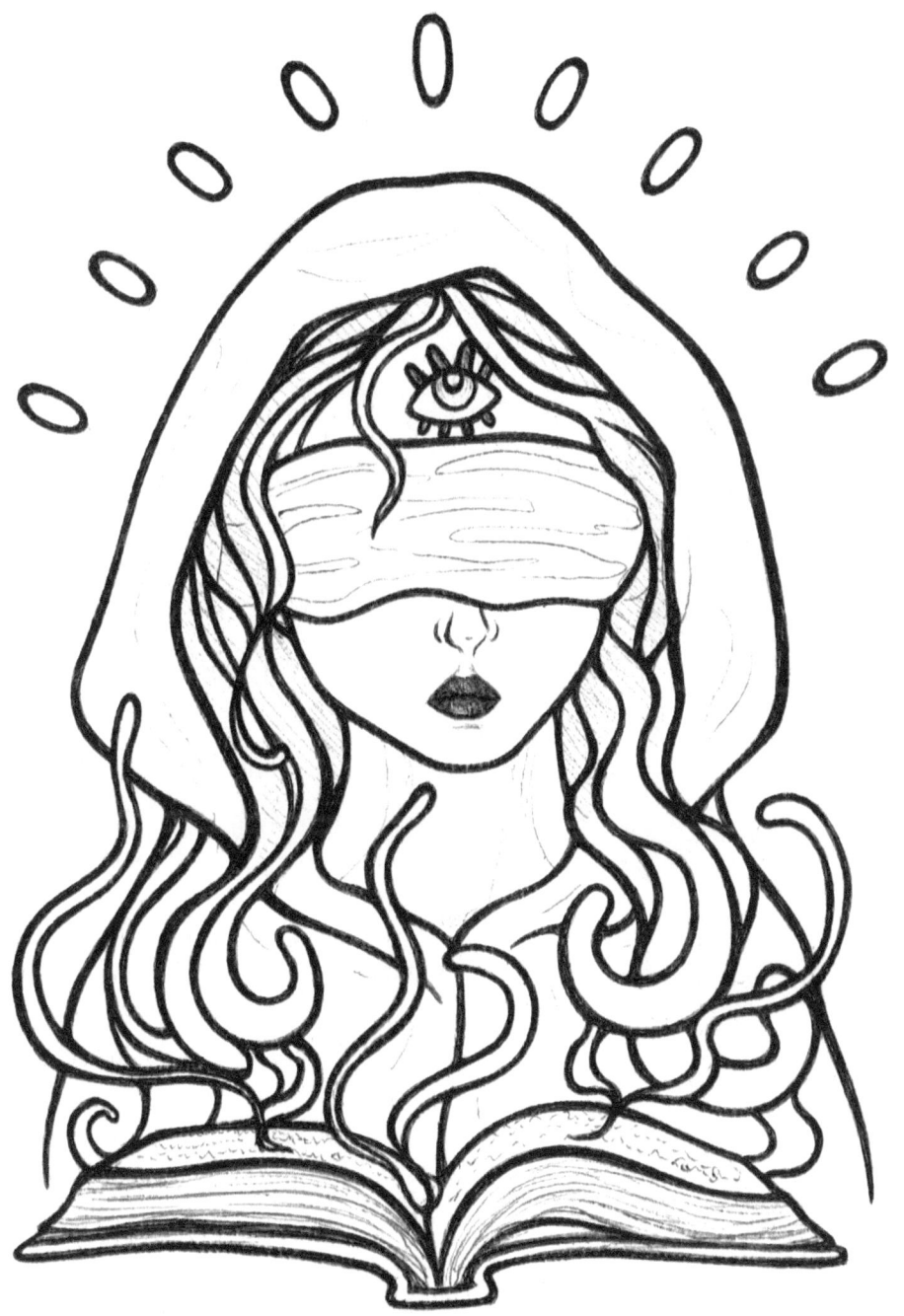

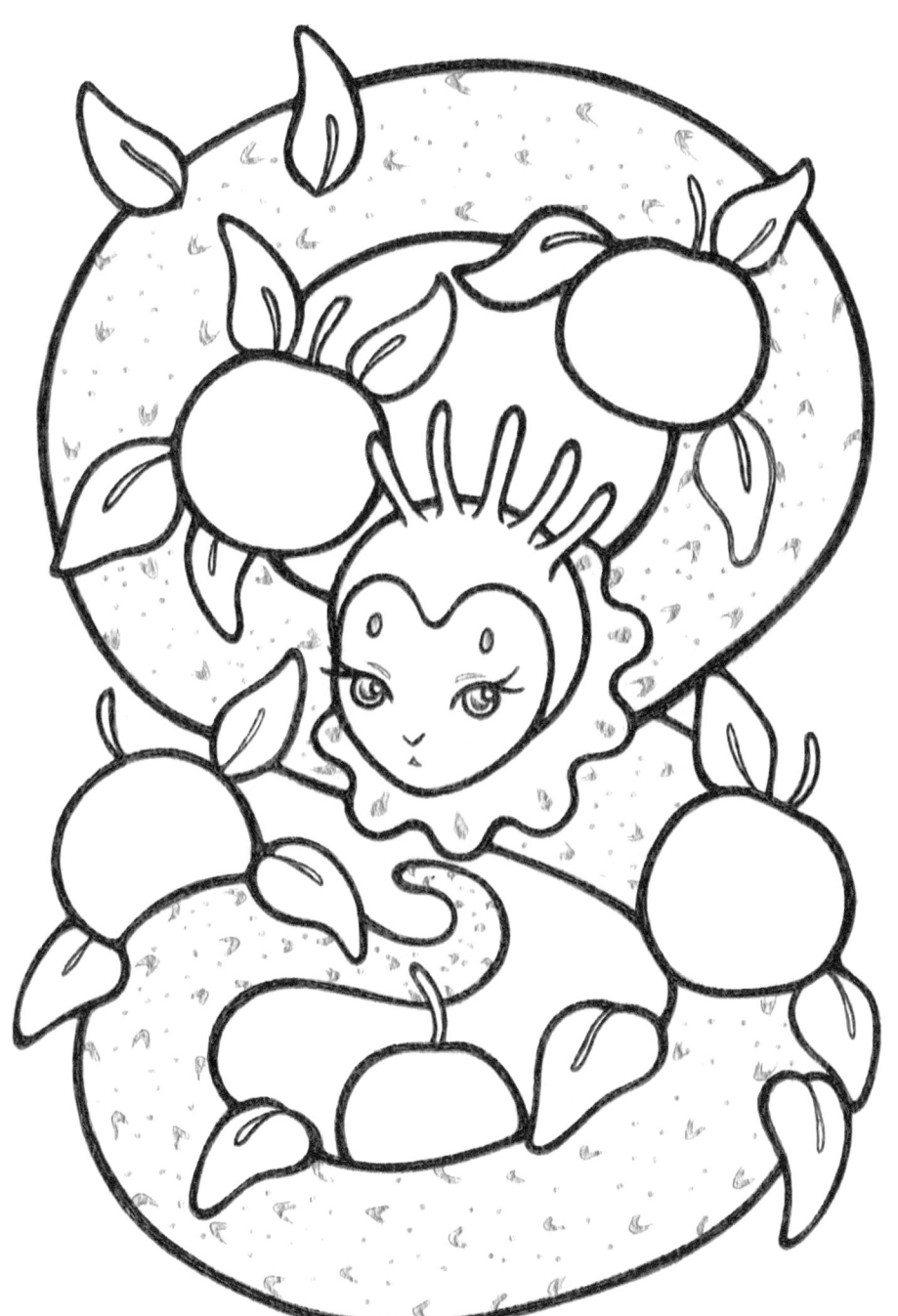

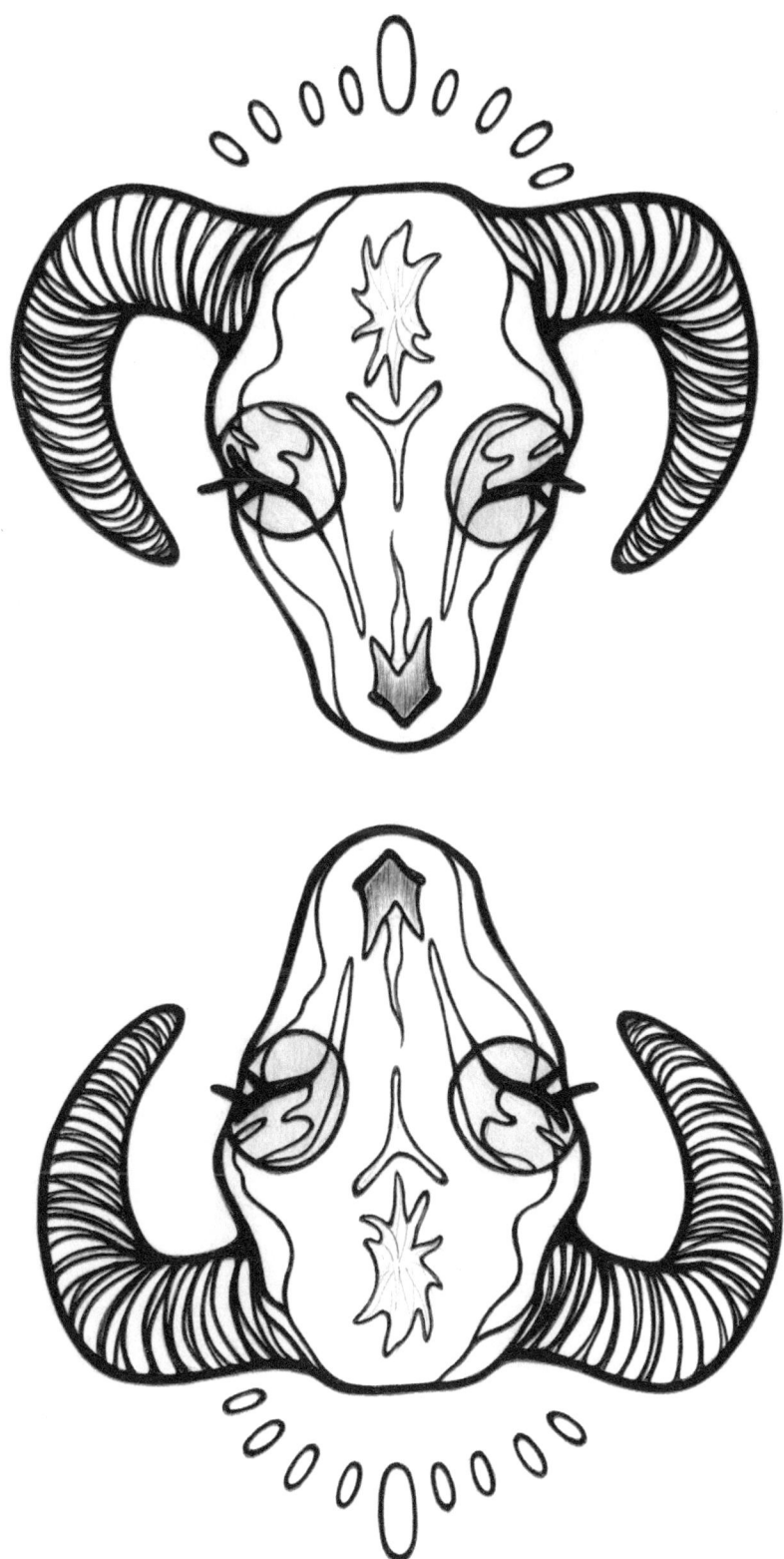

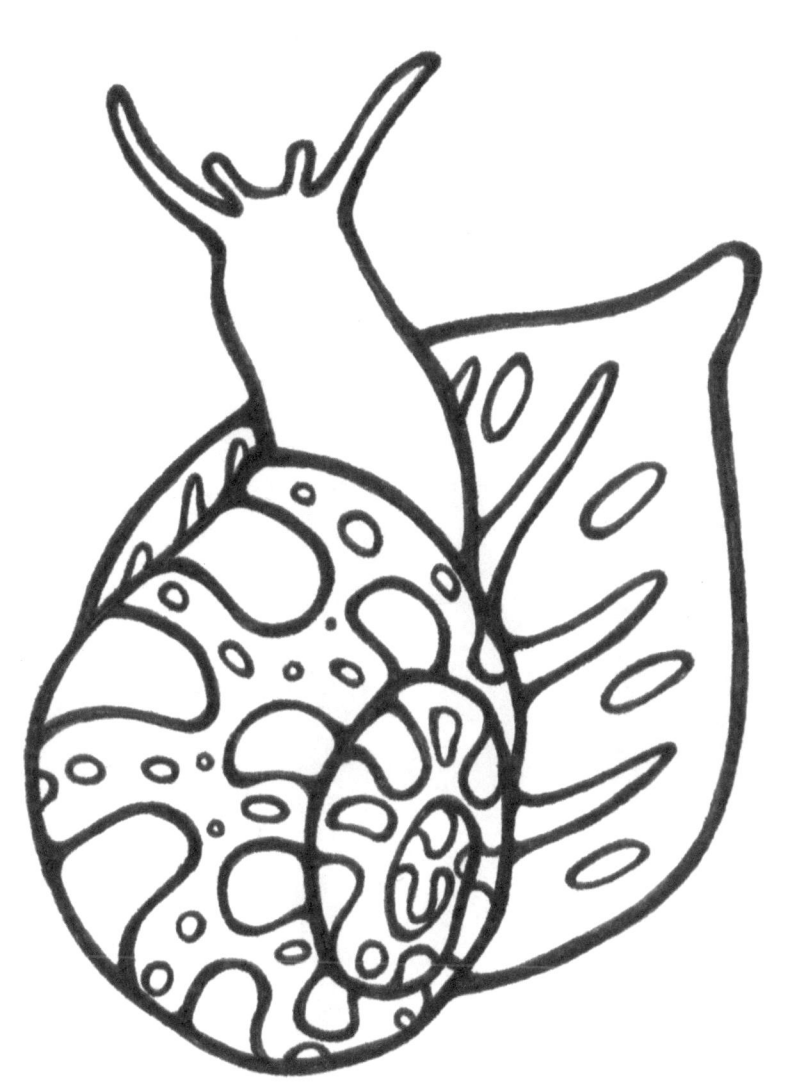

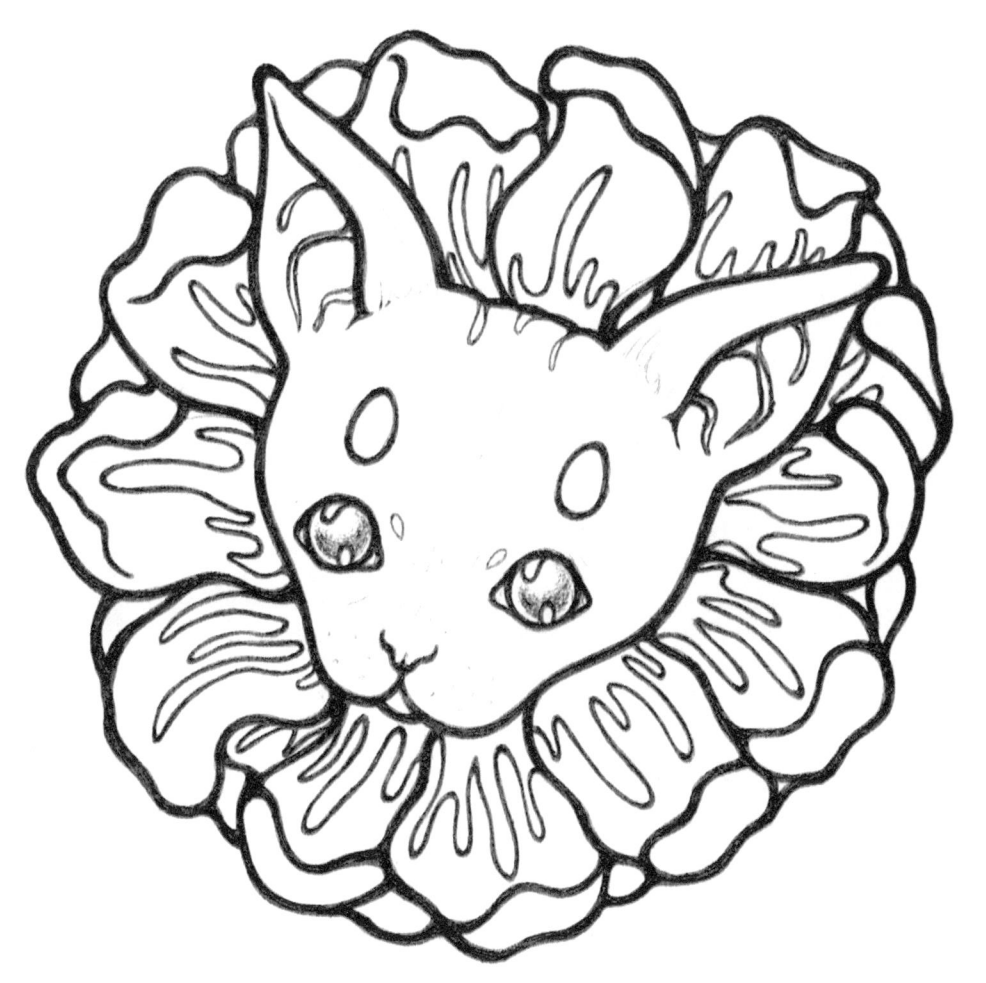

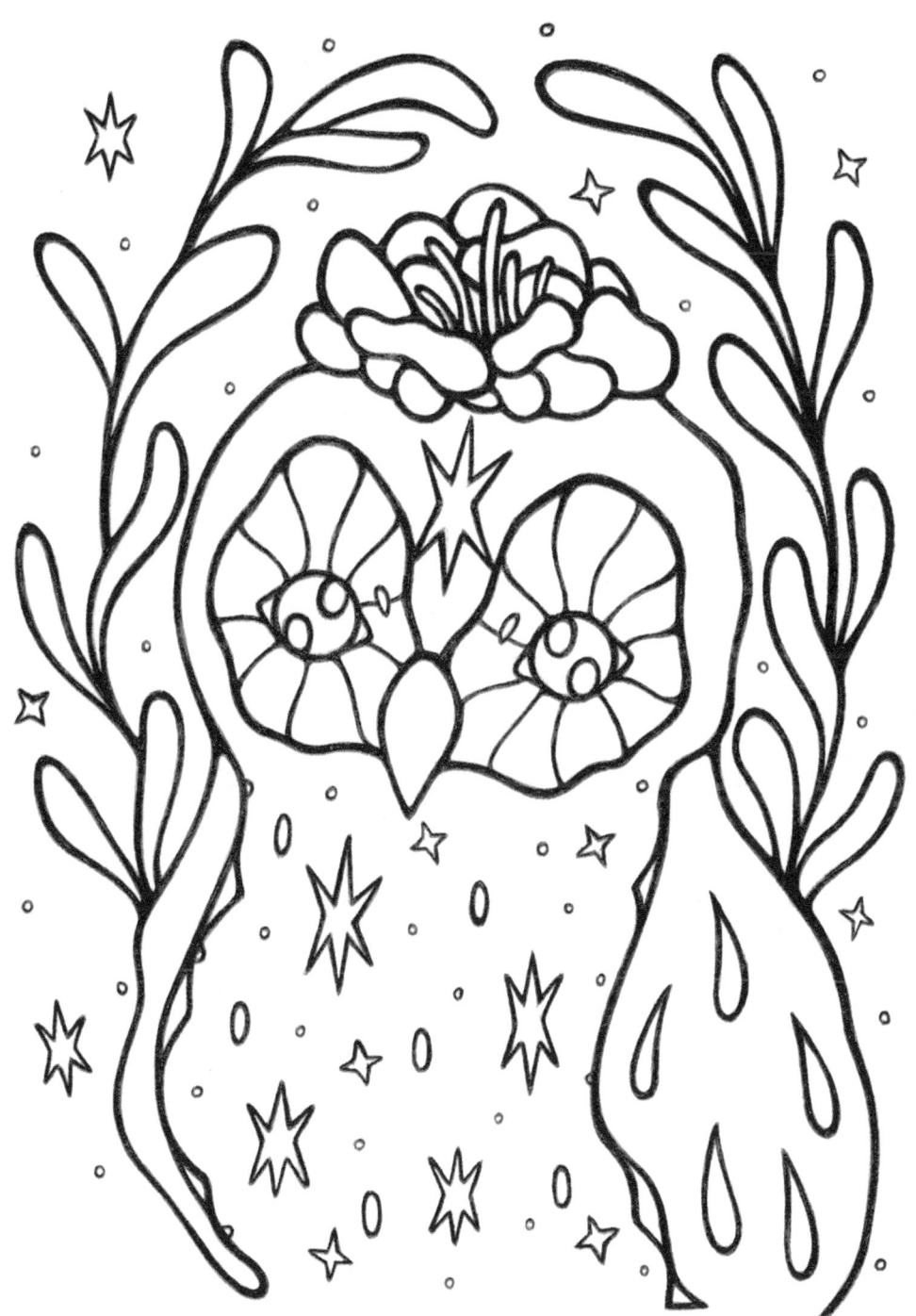

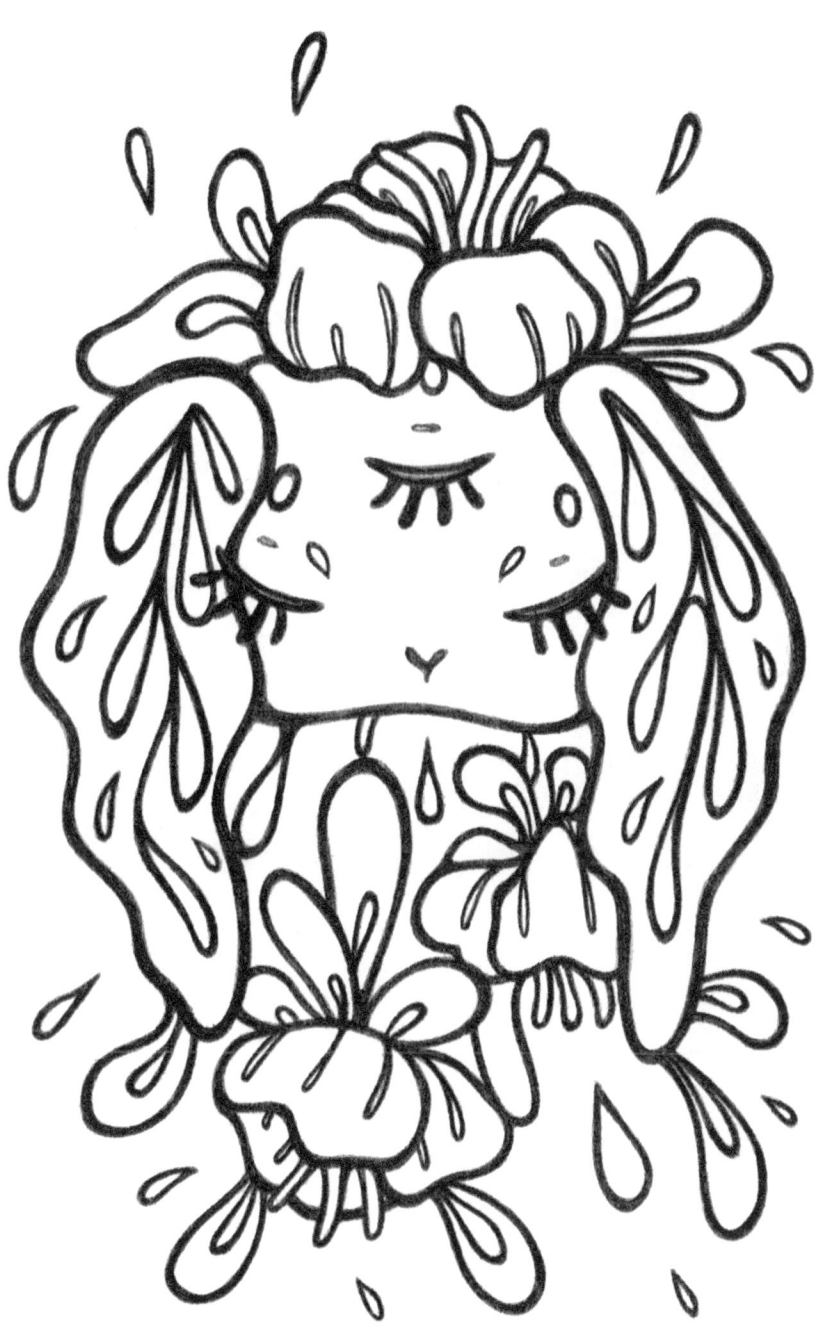

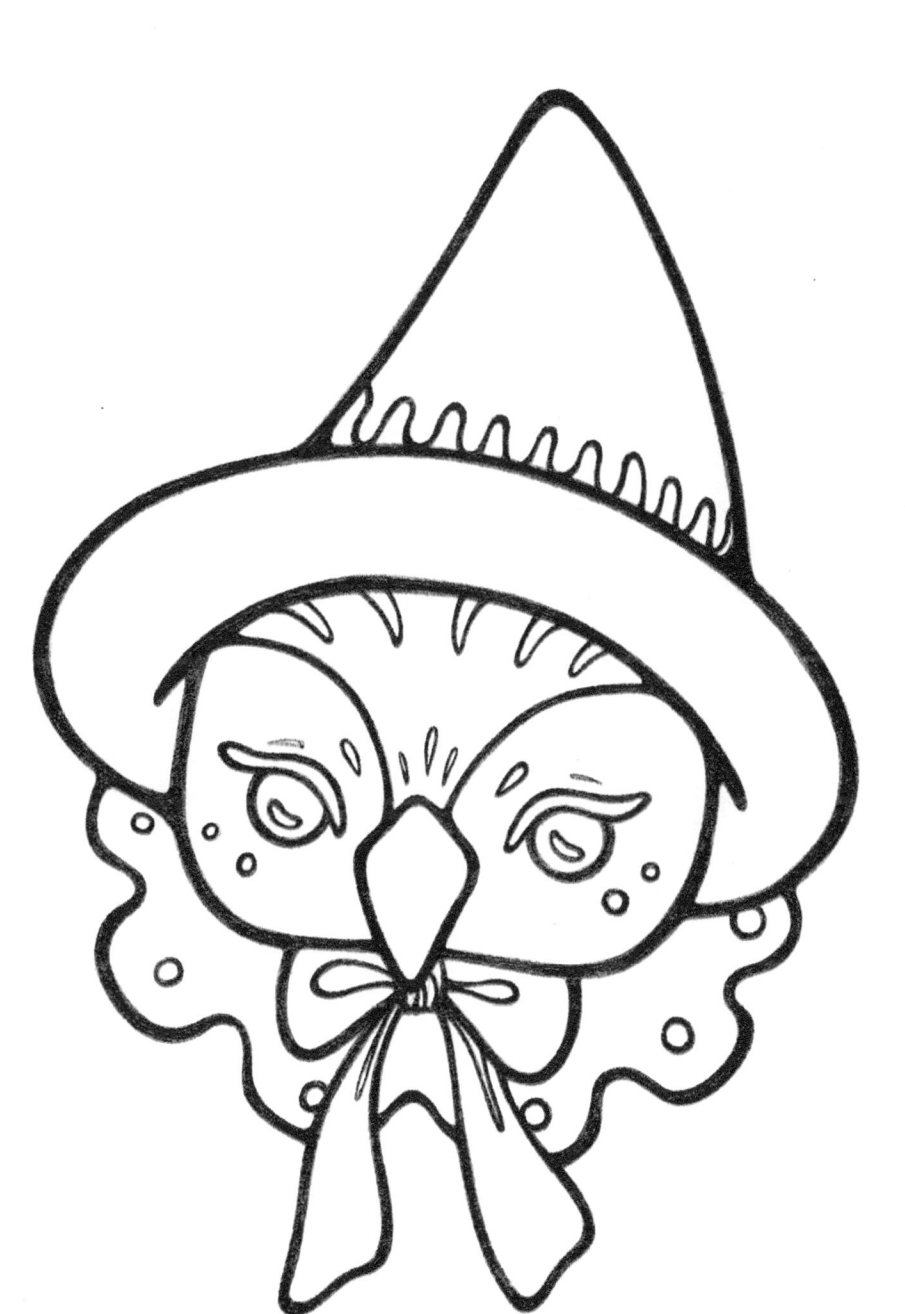